Chevrolet Inline Six-Cylinder

POWER MANUAL

Leo Santucci

California Bill's
Automotive Handbooks

Publishers
Howard Fisher
Helen Fisher

Technical Editor
Tom Wilson

Cover Design
Gary Smith, Performance Design

Book Production
Anne Olson, Casa Cold Type, Inc.
Gary Smith, Performance Design

Front Cover Photo
Howard Fisher

Interior Photography
Teri Santucci, except where noted, with
numerous contributions from members
of Inliners International

Published by
California Bill's Automotive Handbooks
P.O. Box 91858
Tucson, AZ 85752-1858
520-547-2462

Distributed by
Motorbooks International
729 Prospect Avenue
PO Box 1
Osceola, WI 54020-0001
800-826-6600

ISBN
1-931128-15-4

© 2002 California Bill's Automotive Handbooks

Printed in the United States of America

Printing 10 9 8 7 6 5 4 3 2 1

Car shown on front cover, title page and top of back cover belongs to Mike Kirby of Sissell's Automotive. NHRA E/Altered record holder 1966-1969 with driver Kay Sissell. In 1994 and 1996 Mike's son Kevin Kirby drove the car to win Flathead/Inliner points titles becoming the youngest champion in Goodguys history, with a quickest time of 9.26 seconds at 154 MPH. Kevin died of Wegeners disease on June 14, 2000 at age 24. Mike Kirby continues to campaign this car and his dual six-cylinder rail *Sixcession*.

Inliners International is an organization everyone interested in Chevrolet sixes can benefit from greatly. Formed in 1981, its growing membership now totals more than 1,000 members. The organization's *12-Port News* is packed with projects and how-to information. www.inliners.org.

Table of Contents

Leo and Teri Santucci

The author, Tom Langdon and Bill Fisher.

Acknowledgments

When I think of all the Inliners who have helped in seeing this manual to completion, I realize how fortunate I am to have been able to tap into this river of knowledge from so many talented and generous individuals.

I would particularly like to thank the following:

Tom Langdon for his tremendous technical and engineering knowledge that kept me from getting off course.

Pat Smith for his crew chief's eye that kept us from missing the overall picture.

Sarge Nichols for his encouragement and racing knowledge.

Mike Kirby who provided a sounding board and made sure we didn't leave out anything critical.

Ron Sneddon, the "master of CAD" for the beautiful line drawings.

To the many other racers, enthusiasts, engine builders, and shop owners who were generous with their time, thoughts and pictures—they are noted throughout the text.

Last, and certainly not least, I thank my lifelong love, Teri, who has served in every capacity from typist, to pit crew, to editor, to photographer, to dial-in advisor at the track. She is simply the best. Thank you, Queen Bee!

About the Author

The first new car I remember our family getting was a 1954 Chevrolet 2-door hardtop, standard shift, Blue Flame six. I can still see her sitting there in the driveway—turquoise and white, fresh from the factory! I got my driver's license with that car and began working after high school at a local garage where I started to learn about cars and engines. The other mechanic took me to a nearby airport and introduced me to a new sport . . . Drag Racing. I had "the bug"!

My Aunt donated her 1950 Chevy hardtop 235 Powerglide to the cause and I was on my way. (Of course, the Powerglide had to be replaced with a standard shift!) The names Frank McGurk, "California Bill" Fisher and Wayne Horning echoed in my brain.

Over the years, my attention has been on drag racing and always with a Chevy inline six—first the 235, then 261 and now the 292. I've collected just about every article on sixes published in the last thirty years and interviewed many six-cylinder stars such as Kay Sissell, Cotton Perry, Jim Headrick and Glen Self. Yet, I never imagined I'd be the one to put this manual together.

The information contained in this manual is from my own experiences (which are, no doubt, limited), along with corrections, adjustments and additions from longtime six-cylinder enthusiasts Mike Kirby, Tom Langdon, Sarge Nichols and Pat Smith. The information is meant as a starting point for your own departure into sixology.

Of course, it goes without saying, that using the information presented in the manual is without warranty. All the risk for its use is entirely assumed by the user. Good luck on your new adventure!

Chapter 1

Development History

- Confucius once said, "Study the past if you would divine the future." So let's open this manual with the roots of Chevrolet inline sixes—beginning in 1929 and taking you right from pre–WWII to post–WWII to our featured engine series.

Pre–War

Chevrolet introduced its first inline six-cylinder engine (194 CID-cubic inch displacement) in 1929. This engine became the prototype of the refined and rugged four main-bearing block produced from 1937 until 1952. This second generation six-cylinder engine series featured a new head layout, beefed-up block, 3.750" stroke, 3.500" bore, which gave a total displacement of 216 CID. It was quickly dubbed the "Cast Iron Wonder," because most of its parts, including pistons, were made of cast iron.

In 1941, a Hi-Torque version appeared for use in large trucks; the thicker cylinder walls and a new bore (3.562") and stroke (3.937") produced 235 CID. It was manufactured until 1949. This engine used a full-length pushrod and side head cover and should not be confused with later 235 passenger car engines.

Post–War

With the introduction of Chevrolet's Powerglide torque converter transmission in 1950, a need for more power in the passenger car resulted in a new version of the truck Hi-Torque. This new engine featured a higher block casting and

1929 Chevrolet Inline Six—the first of a long line that would go uninterrupted for over sixty years! This first six displaced 194 CID. Copyright 1978 GM Corporation. Used with permission of GM Media Archives.

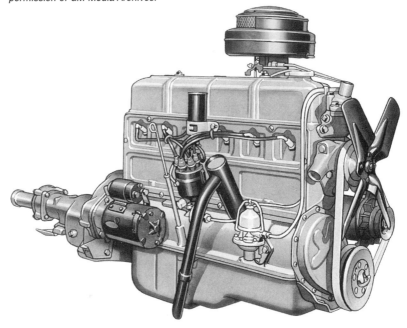

The "Cast Iron Wonder"—216 CID 1937–1952 and 1941–1949 high torque 235 CID. These engines are identified by their full pushrod side cover and two attaching studs through ribbed valve cover. The 216 and 235 can be separated by bore and stroke differences. Copyright 1978 GM Corporation. Used with permission of GM Media Archives.

The new 235 CID High Torque and 261 CID Job Master. 1950–1962 passenger car (235) and heavy duty truck 1954–1962 (261). Notice the partial pushrod side cover and 4 screw valve cover attachment. Copyright 1978 GM Corporation. Used with permission of GM Media Archives.

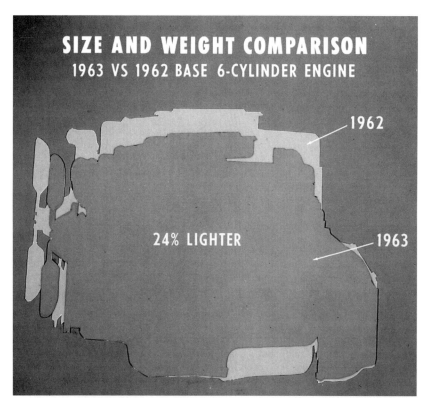

SIZE AND WEIGHT COMPARISON
1963 VS 1962 BASE 6-CYLINDER ENGINE

1962

24% LIGHTER

1963

1962 235–261 CID vs 1963 194-250 CID. The 1963 292 CID is approximately the same height as the 235–261 CID and about 19% lighter. Length is the same as the 194-250 CID. Copyright 1978 GM Corporation. Used with permission of GM Media Archives.

redesigned head with larger valves. The block had only a partial length pushrod side cover; that is, it did not extend beyond the top of the block onto the head itself as the earlier designs did.

The same bore (3.562") and stroke (3.937") produced the 235 CID "Powerglide version". The 216 continued as the basic engine with standard transmission.

By 1954, the 235 "Powerglide version" had become Chevrolet's Standard (passenger car) engine. These 235s featured aluminum pistons, full pressure oiling and durability that earned them praise and respect throughout the automotive world. It was a versatile engine, at home on Main Street going to the grocery store, or, when highly modified, holding its own by finishing third in a highly competitive field of V8s at Pike's Peak Hill Climb during the late '50s.

In 1954, Chevrolet introduced a new version of the Hi-Torque for use in large trucks (it was also later used in Canadian passenger cars). This was to be the last and largest version in this engine series. It became known as the Job Master 261; cast of a high strength close grained alloy, with a bore of 3.750" and stroke of 3.937" resulting in a displacement of 261 cubic inches. This engine lived up to and surpassed its predecessors. Its lightweight, rugged construction, hi-torque and full interchangeability with passenger 235s made it a favorite among stock car, sportsman and drag racers alike.

The year 1962 saw the last production for this famous six. Weight reduction, new lower body styles, smaller cars, more advanced engine technology, as well as the desire to develop more assembly-line interchangeability with Chevrolet's new V8, finally terminated the engine series.

Cutaway version of the 194-250 CID. Notice pushrod covers (height of 4"). Fuel pump is adjacent to the distributor and the motor mount is about in the center of the block (not shown in cutaway). Copyright 1978 GM Corporation. Used with permission of GM Media Archives.

Featured Series

Chevrolet introduced its next inline six series in 1962. This was cast in a new thin wall design and became available first in the Chevy II and Nova models providing 194 cubic inches (3.563" bore x 3.250" stroke). The standard passenger car line began with the 1963 model year 230 CID engine, featuring a bore of 3.875" and a stroke of 3.250". Beginning in 1965, the Chevy II and Chevelle series were also available with the 230 CID engine.

It should also be mentioned that Pontiac used a version (not OHC) of this engine in the Tempest (1963 only). It was 215 cu. in. with a bore of 3.750" and a stroke of 3.250". In 1967, Chevrolet began offering a larger version of the 230 CID engine providing 250 CID; the bore remained 3.875" while the stroke increased to 3.530". This engine became the standard inline six with the 1971 model year, both in the full size and intermediate passenger car lines.

Chevrolet also produced a cast iron four cylinder of 153 cu. in. (3.875" bore x 3.250" stroke) derived from the basic six cylinder configuration. This engine was used in relatively

153 CID (four cylinder) Notice the strong family resemblance! Copyright 1978 GM Corporation. Used with permission of GM Media Archives.

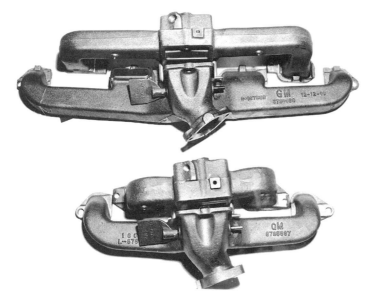

194-250 CID and 153 CID (four cylinder) intake/exhaust manifold comparison. Copyright 1978 GM Corporation. Used with permission of GM Media Archives.

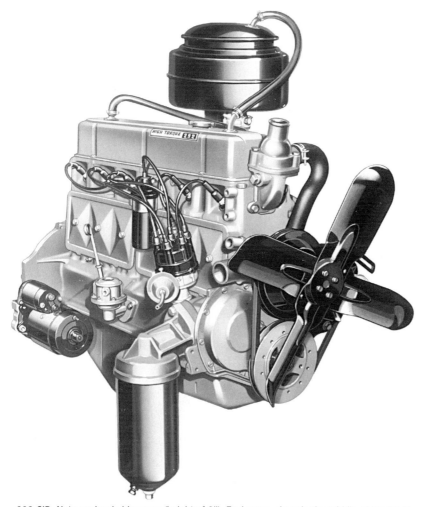

292 CID. Note pushrod side cover (height of 6"). Fuel pump about in the middle of the block. Motor mount adjacent to the distributor not visible in this picture due to 90° oil filter adapter used exclusively in large trucks. Block deck height 1.75" higher than the 194-250 CID series. Copyright 1978 GM Corporation. Used with permission of GM Media Archives.

small numbers in both the Chevy II and Nova from 1962–1971. It shared many parts with its bigger brothers (including head design with Siamesed intake ports). GM later used this engine as the basis for its 2.5 liter "Iron Duke" series, most recently adapting it to a transverse mounting in front wheel drive application.

Chevrolet introduced the largest, and perhaps the best, six—the 292 CID (3.875" bore x 4.120" stroke) engine—beginning in the 1963 model year. The 292 CID was produced only for truck use and became the common engine of both the Chevrolet and GMC lines. It has gone on to prove itself, when properly modified, to be the "big block" six of its era. Nothing could out-torque or out-horsepower it, so it didn't take long for this engine to become a favorite transplant candidate into the passenger car line by wily hot rodders.

Chapter 2

Planning Your Project

- How to plan an inline project
- Theories and formulas about how to make horsepower

So now that you've made the decision to take "the path less traveled" and build a unique inline six, the question becomes "where do I start?"

Before jumping into the nuts and bolts, so to speak, it is always worth your time to thoroughly contemplate a proposed plan of action for your engine.

Setting Goals

The questions you need to ask yourself are:

1. Will I want this engine for street, strip, oval track, or...?
2. What particular attributes will my engine need for my use—be it street, drags, oval track, hill climb, sports or swamp buggy?
3. What weight vehicle will the engine need to propel?
4. Do I have a realistic budget for this project?
5. Can I reasonably expect to make enough horsepower and torque to achieve my goals?
6. At my projected horsepower level, can I expect reasonable engine life?

Jack of all trades, master of none is a phrase that could easily apply to an engine. The reason is a simple one. As we modify an engine to a specific task, it requires compromise in another area. Every change in one direction produces an effect in another. For example, a full race cam will produce great top-end power but will extract a woeful effect on low-speed performance. On the other hand, a good low RPM torque cam will be next to useless for high RPM racing situations. This is why dual purpose engines are counter-productive. Decide now or lament later!

Once you know what specific purpose you are building the engine for—then you need to emphasize those characteristics most desirable for the project. If you build an engine for hill-climbing, you want to emphasize low-end torque production—a much different theme than a high RPM drag strip engine.

When you think about performance, you also have to consider the vehicle weight. Generally, the heavier the vehicle, the more power is required to move the vehicle, thus adding more stress to the engine. Therefore you should always build as light as either feasible or allowable under the prevailing rules for your application.

You need to have an adequate budget to purchase the right parts. If you don't—do not proceed! Be smart. Save so you can do it right—the first time.

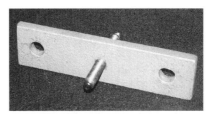

Homemade piston stop, stock-type head. Note elongated holes (due to head bolt spacing variations).

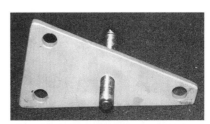

The second piston stop is for use with the hybrid Chevy V8 head bolt pattern.

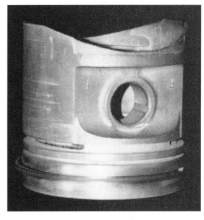

Homemade piston ring squaring tool, simply an old piston with the compression ring in place. Invert the piston, place ring in the cylinder and push down until the compression ring on the piston stops against the block. Remove the piston and measure the ring gap.

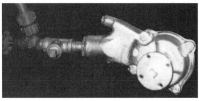

Block integrity tester is made by epoxying the inlet spigot to an old water pump. It is used in conjunction with a gasket and torque plate in order to pressure test any potential block.

Crankshaft turning tool—for use with a degree wheel. Several variations of this tool exist, take your pick (whatever fits the small block Chevy V8 fits both inline six series engines).

Harmonic balancer installation and removal kit. Never EVER think of installing the harmonic balancer any other way! Hammering on a harmonic damper can damage its rubber isolating ring leading to a potentially catastrophic separation later.

Homemade tool cut from an old flex plate to lock the engine to torque either the flywheel or harmonic balancer retaining bolt when the cylinder head is on.

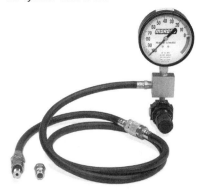

The leak down tester uses compressed air to verify piston and valve sealing conditions.

If you don't, you'll wind up doing it over, and paying twice.

Plan conservatively when contemplating horsepower and torque levels. Don't expect a mildly configured engine to suddenly come alive with the addition of a 200 HP nitrous kit. It more likely will come to a sudden death.

Finally, if the engine will produce, let's say 500 HP, be sure all the components have been sufficiently upgraded to handle this power level. Conversely, if the engine needs to produce only 250 HP, then most stock components will be adequate. Upgrading beyond stock would simply be a waste of your resources.

Remember, a problem well stated is half-solved. So, spend your time making sure you have set realistic goals for your engine and chassis before you plunge in.

Paths to Power

Along these lines, let's review what Roger Huntington used to call *The Paths to Power*. Here I've updated the basic five paths Roger described. They are as valid today as they were when he wrote about them in the late forties and early fifties. If we want to make more power and torque, we can:

1. Increase the piston displacement (read cubic inches/liters). You accomplish this by either boring the cylinders larger or increasing the length of the stroke—or both.

2. Increase the weight of the charge inducted. Here you want to supply the engine with cool air (ducted) from outside the engine bay and cool the fuel with a cool can. This allows a denser mixture.

You could also use a fuel other than gasoline, one with a higher latent heat such as alcohol. You might also use a fuel that carries more oxygen with it, such as nitromethane. You can even inject nitrous oxide into the gasoline mixture and achieve a similar result. Of course, to get more fuel and air in, you'd want to port and polish (airflow) the head and use a high performance intake system. You can also add more carburetion (or increase the capacity of the fuel injection system), as well as putting in a longer duration, higher lift camshaft. Last, but not least, you can force more air by either supercharging or turbocharging.

3. Increase the efficiency of combustion. Here, you can raise the compression ratio and alter the deck height of the block to obtain proper squish or quench. (This is the area that creates turbulence in a wedge style cylinder head. It is this turbulence that creates a more complete combustion.) Proper piston design, along with an optimum fuel-air mixture and an efficient ignition system also works. You need to remember not only to burn the mixture, but also to get rid of it with a properly designed exhaust system.

4. Increase the RPM/HP curve. The reason why we can gain power by increasing the RPM is that we can generate more power strokes within a given time frame. Today, there are special lightweight pistons, pins, rods, pushrods, rocker arms and valve spring retainers. You can also lighten the crankshaft, harmonic balancer, flywheel or flexplate. Any of these changes allow you to use a camshaft that will produce more horsepower at the top end. Along with this, you need to be sure everything is in perfect balance.

5. Decrease friction and pumping losses. Of course, you need adequate lubrication at all times—the higher the RPM the more oil pressure is needed. You can also use special coatings on pistons, valves, the crank, as well as use synthetic motor oil. You might also want to increase the bearing clearances slightly to provide a greater cushion between parts and you want to control where the oil gets thrown—a modified oil pan with crank scrapers, pan baffles and side kick out. You may even try a dry sump oiling system.

Finally, you need a proper exhaust system to eliminate back pressure and complement your intake system and camshaft timing to maximize power.

Another way to view making horsepower in an internal combustion engine is to look more closely at the underlying formulas that determine this power. This allows you to choose the most appropriate modifications for your application.

Bear in mind inline engines

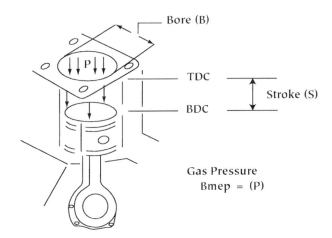

POWER PRODUCTION

$$HP = \frac{TORQUE \times RPM}{5252}$$

TORQUE = PLA
P = BREAK MEAN EFFECTIVE PRESSURE (Bmep)
LA = DISPLACEMENT (D)
D = 4.72 X Stroke X Bore ^{2}
(L6 CYLINDER DISPLACEMENT)

Power production—horsepower formula.

were engineered to be high torque/low RPM machines. It is important for you to not only recognize these facts, but also to utilize them when you modify your engine for high output.

Power Formula

Horsepower is described by the following formula:

HP = (Torque x RPM)/5252

Horsepower is a way to express how much work an engine can do. Work is really equal to force times distance. Notice in our horsepower formula that torque is the force. Torque being the twisting force

of the crankshaft that gets applied to the rest of the drive line. Revolutions per minute (RPM) is the distance traveled by our crankshaft. The number 5252 converts this information into units of measurement. So let's look at what makes up torque.

T = **PLA**

P = brake mean effective pressure or the pressure pushing the piston down the cylinder bore.
L = length of the stroke.
A = size of the bore.
LA = D = displacement.
D = 4.72 x stroke x bore^2= six cylinder engine displacement in cubic inches.

Torque plate—shown as dual pattern for stock bolt pattern and also for hybrid head (Chevy V8).

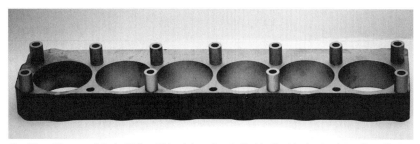

Traditional torque plate by Yother. This plate, when bolted to the block, simulates the effect on the bore when the cylinder head is bolted on. Note spacers added to top of plate. This allows the use of stock-length bolt or stud, which simplifies using this plate. A thick plate is necessary to duplicate stresses created by the cylinder head.

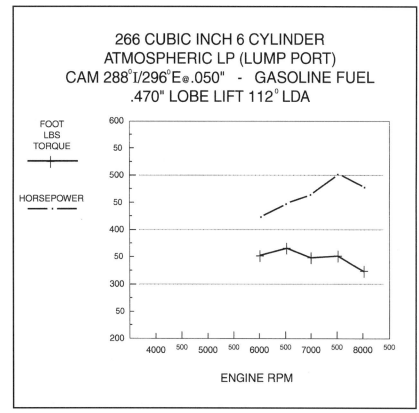

266 CUBIC INCH 6 CYLINDER ATMOSPHERIC LP (LUMP PORT)
CAM 288°I/296°E@.050" - GASOLINE FUEL
.470" LOBE LIFT 112° LDA

Self Racing Heads & Engines' STD-LD dyno-graph lump port stock-type head.

Discussion

We see in our formula that displacement is one of the two ways to increase torque at all RPM ranges. Before we talk about the second way to achieve this, let's see what increasing displacement does for power.

By looking at the formula, we can see that increasing the bore will give the maximum value for the money. In fact, tests have shown that while a .125" increase in bore can add about a 10 percent increase in power, the same .125" increase in stroke yields only about one half that amount. Besides, there are physical limits to increasing D and it goes without saying that to achieve even these gains, you need to improve volumetric efficiency proportionally.

The second way to increase torque is to increase the P (bmep). In a naturally aspirated (atmospheric) engine, this can be achieved by increasing the compression ratio while maintaining the highest average cylinder pressure through proper cam timing and cylinder sealing. We could also introduce a fuel that carries more oxygen than gasoline, such as methanol, nitrous oxide or nitromethane. In a supercharged or turbocharged engine, this is achieved by increasing the boost pressure available.

Now let's talk about the role of RPM for a minute. We could make more horsepower by increasing RPM, but we have already said inlines are not created to be RPM machines. Limits exist due to the long crankshafts and inherent imbalance of the design.

Remember: Loads on the rods and pistons increase as the square of the RPM. This means that when you raise the RPM to create more horsepower, for example, by going from 6,000 RPM to

7,200 RPM, you increase the loads by 44 percent! It is easy to see that, even using the best rods and pistons, this avenue will lead to increased parts breakage.

Looking at the big picture, where does this leave you? The most highly modified competition inline atmospheric engines of this design can achieve a maximum power level of about 2.3 times displacement. This translates into 593 HP for a typical "250" + .060 over = 258 CID and 695 HP for a "292" + .060 over = 302 CID engine. The modifications necessary to create these extreme power levels are only compatible with full competition usage.

So what are the practical street level limits on gasoline? These are on the order of 1.1 times displacement or 284 HP and 332 HP respectively. Bear in mind, even these are substantial horsepower increases and require compromises in drivability.

Drivability is created by reasonable RPM limits (small intake ports, conservative camshaft profiles and high velocity intake systems). This is the exact opposite of what we do to create power with atmospheric—naturally aspirated—engines!

Conclusion

The formula T = PLA shows the best method to gain HP is to increase P through forced induction and here adiabatic (heat) efficiency weighs heavily towards turbocharged engines or nitrous oxide systems. The best thing about this is that inline engines are a near perfect match for the project. A properly forced induction engine has a short duration, low overlap cam design, port sizes on the small side for high velocity at low speeds, strong bottom end (seven main bearings) and a moderate

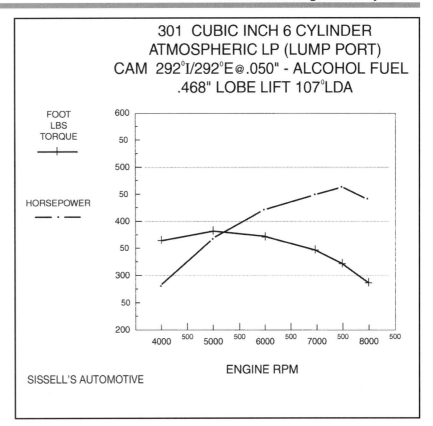

Sissell's Automotive HD-TD dyno-graph lump port stock-type head.

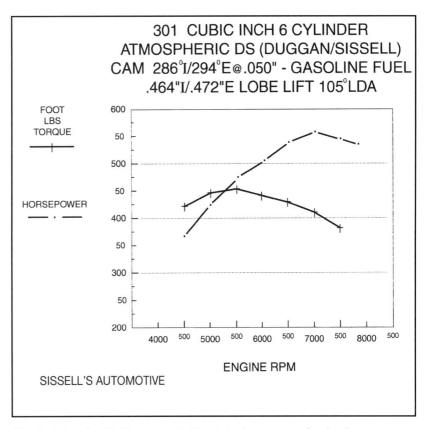

Sissell's Automotive HD-TD dyno-graph 12 port aluminum noncrossflow head.

Mike Kirby at the Sissell dyno searching for more horsepower.

Camshaft degreeing kit with a 12-inch diameter degree wheel. The larger wheel is substituted for the standard 9-inch diameter for greater accuracy.

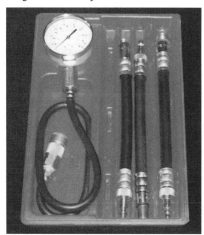

A compression gauge gives a good indication of the dynamic seal of the engine (valves and piston rings).

Strobe timing light allows accurate setting of total timing.

RPM range, typically 6,000 RPM or less.

What kind of horsepower can be made? With a nitrous system, you could add 200+ HP for short durations. With a turbocharged engine, no one really knows the limit. Purpose-built Grand Prix turbocharged engines produce horsepower of 15 times displacement!

Practical street power at only six pounds boost (see chart page 140) could average 344 HP for the 258 CID and 402 HP for the 301 CID—definitely worth a second and third look, wouldn't you say?

Critical Parts

When all is said and done, if you plan to run a healthy Chevy six, the most critical parts you will need are:

For Longevity:
1. Torsional damper (Harmonic Balancer) i.e., Fluidampr, ATI, Fisher, etc.
2. Aluminum rods for drag racing. Upgraded steel rods for the street. Custom steel rods for oval track.

For Power and Torque:
3. Precision head work.
4. Proper camshaft design.

You will need to allocate your available dollars to these areas first.

DON'T SKIMP HERE!
Once you have decided on your plan, there are several tools that you need to make or buy that will greatly aid in the proper building and tuning of your engine.

Important Tools

Consider this a basic list for building a serious inline engine:

1. Positive piston stop.
2. Piston ring squaring tool.
3. Block and head integrity tester.
4. Harmonic balancer installation and removal tool.
5. Flywheel locking tool.
6. Crankshaft turning tool.
7. Torque plate for boring and honing.
8. Engine leak down tester.
9. Dial indicator with magnetic base and degree wheel (minimum 9-inch diameter).
10. Compression gauge.
11. Timing light.

Not included in this list are standard rebuilding tools.

Chapter 3

Block Indentification and Selection

- How to identify various blocks available
- How to select the best block for your project
- How to find defects in the casting
- Additional tests to ensure a solid block

All of this series of the Chevrolet/GMC inline sixes have the same width and length dimensions. All the 194, 215, 230 and 250 CID also have identical height dimensions, consequently, we'll refer to these as the Standard Low Deck (STD-LD) series engines.

These engines are fully interchangeable with minor modifications or proper block selection.

Now you can start to see the beauty of Chevrolet/GMC. The back of the inline six is also identical to the Chevy V8— allowing full interchangeability of bell housing, transmission, flywheels, etc.

Where to Start

Our horsepower formula reminds us that one of the quickest ways to gain power is to increase displacement. So, if you have a 194 CID Nova, just bolt in a 250 CID engine. Or, why not use a 292 CID engine (we'll refer to these as the Heavy Duty Tall Deck (HD-TD block series). There are really only a few reasons why you wouldn't consider this option:

1. You are limited by race association rules. Horsepower to weight rules favor small engines,

Bell housing side of L6 HD-TD.

Bell housing side of small block Chevy V8—identical.

Bell housing side L6 STD-LD.

Front view HD-TD.

Front view STD-LD.

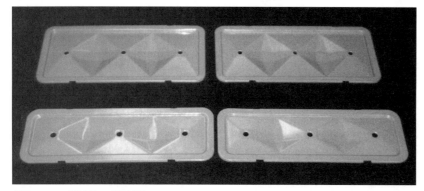

Side covers HD-TD vs STD-LD.

Identification

Externally, the HD-TD can be easily identified by its high block profile and tall pushrod side covers (6") as compared to the STD-LD six-cylinder series (4").

The factory casting itself is a compact, lightweight (151 lbs. bare), rugged, seven main bearing design. The external dimensions are identical to the smaller six cylinders to the exception of requiring about 1.750" of additional hood clearance and a relocated motor mount on the passenger side of the block from roughly a centered position to one adjacent to the distributor area. With these simple changes the engine is a "natural" for instant horsepower updating in most STD-LD inline six cylinder Chevrolet passenger cars and trucks.

There is an old saying in racing: "You can't beat cubic inches except with cubic money." It is for this reason that this manual will deal primarily with the 40+ cu. in. larger HD-TD block; although most of these tips will also apply to the STD-LD series as well. Any significant differences will be noted.

Where to Find

The HD-TD is widely available and commonly found in 3/4-ton pickup trucks (Chevy and GMC) from 1963 through 1988, as well as in larger models of both makes. The block can also be ordered new (currently made in Mexico) from Chevrolet or GMC as a Goodwrench 4.8L complete Engine Assembly under part #10121028 (includes assembled long block, head, crankshaft, camshaft, timing gears, pistons, connecting rods, side covers, timing cover, oil pump, pick-up and oil pan).

because they produce more horsepower per cubic inch.
2. Your chassis and hood clearance won't support the extra height of the HD-TD.
3. Price or availability puts the HD-TD out of reach.

If you can, go to the HD-TD engine. It costs no more to build and gives you a substantial increase in both power and torque.

Inspection

There seems to be no particular year or series that is structurally superior, although many racers favor the early model years (1963–71), and others favor the Mexican-made block. The block casting is of a "thin wall" design, therefore, it is very important to check any used block very carefully. I would suggest a thorough pressure cleaning followed by a visual inspection starting with the block deck surface, the sides, front and back. Be sure to look at the main bearing webs, caps, between cylinders and lifter bores.

This is also the time to reject blocks with obviously shifted cylinder cores. If you look at the front of the block where the water pump body inserts, you are looking at the number 1 cylinder wall. The best blocks have a machined clearance for the water pump impeller that runs vertically and is 3/8" wide. Still, if sonic testing is available, it is easily the most accurate way to identify poorly cast blocks.

If the block passes this inspection, mark all main bearing caps for location. Hot tank and subject the block to magnaflux and pressure testing before committing the expensive machining operations necessary to turn this plentiful truck engine into a potent V8 threat.

Final Block Tips

1. The back of the Chevy/GMC 6 block, whether HD-TD or the STD-LD series, is identical to the Chevy V8 block so that bell housings, transmissions, etc., are completely interchangeable.
2. Use solid motor mounts for full race applications. Motor plates are preferred for the STD-LD series; conventional mounts may induce vibration

Passenger side HD-TD.

Driver side HD-TD.

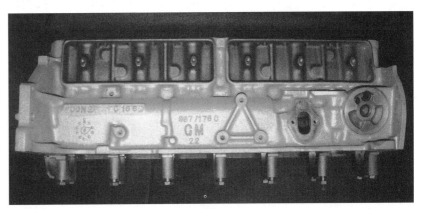

Passenger side STD-LD. Note motor mount and fuel pump location differences.

Driver side STD-LD.

Block casting number 377129 GM, 21 mold number, CON 2 indicates conveyor number 2 moved the block, F128 the letter indicates the month, day and year the block was cast. In this case, June 12. The year was 8, the decade probably 1988 (because this block had no timing gear oiler). The clock-like raised positions indicate shift and time the block was cast.

The numbers stamped into the distributor pad indicate where the block was cast and its dress (what compression ratio and accessories it had).

cracks along the lifter gallery.

3. Make a low cost block integrity tester with an old water pump housing. Epoxy plumbing fittings in large hose end. Seal closed small heater hose opening. Attach valve (available from a plumbing supply house) and pressure gauge. When used in conjunction with a torque plate, household water pressure (hot) will quickly detect hidden leaks in the block casting. This unit can save a lot of heartache when considering a used casting!

4. Use the most inexpensive spray paint when finishing the exterior of the block.

5. The weak areas of both series blocks are the corner holes, especially the STD-LD front driver side hole.

Head casting number.

Mexican HD-TD block.

Typical pickup where you would find an HD-TD.

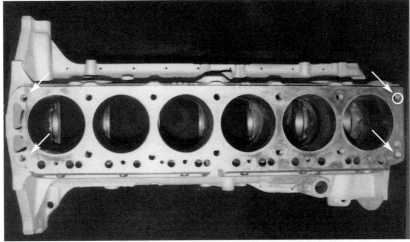

Deck surface—corner holes are the ones most likely to show cracks—especially STD-LD front driver side hole (circle).

On driver side of block look for cracks around core (freeze) plugs.

The deck surface of the block is thin here and one of the water pump mounting holes is closely adjacent. When high compression ratios are used with these engines, this area is usually the first to show cracks. Because of this weakness, it should be noted that head gasket manufacturers often quote a different torque figure for this bolt. The HD-TD block has a much higher deck height and therefore does not suffer the same degree of weakness.

Pressure testing fixture.

Note width of water pump machined clearance. Best width 3/8" and even. Note (arrow) taper present on this block. This indicates core shift during casting.

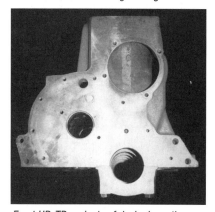

Front HD-TD—plenty of deck above the water pump opening.

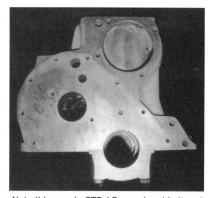

Note thinness in STD-LD near head bolt and water pump opening. This is weakest head bolt area on STD-LD.

Enlarged view of head bolt area as seen through the water pump opening.

Basic Engine Specifications

Bore	194 CID	3.563"
	215 CID (Pontiac)	3.750"
	230 CID	3.875"
	250 CID	3.875"
	292 CID	3.875"
Stroke	194 CID	3.250"
	215 CID (Pontiac)	3.250"
	230 CID	3.250"
	250 CID	3.530"
	292 CID	4.120" +/- .005"*
Displacement	As designated	
Numbering system		
Front to Rear	1-2-3-4-5-6	
Firing Order	1-5-3-6-2-4	
Distributor Rotation	Clockwise (as viewed from the top)	
Number of Main Bearings	7	
Location of Thrust Bearing	Rear Main	
Crankshaft Main Bearing Diameter		2.298"
Rod Journal Diameter	194–250 CID	2.000"
	292 CID	2.100"
Connecting Rod Length	194 CID	5.700"
	215 CID (Pontiac)	5.700"
	230 CID	5.700"
	250 CID	5.700"
	292 CID	6.760" +/- .003"
Piston Compression Height	194 CID	1.795"
	215 CID (Pontiac)	1.795"
	230 CID	1.795"
	250 CID	1.655"
	292 CID	2.025"
Block Deck Height	STD-LD	9.150" +/- .007"
	HD-TD	10.875" +/- .007"
Valve Head Diameter	All Engines	
Inlet		1.720"
Exhaust		1.500"

*This is usually noted as 4.125". (Racers like to claim every last inch of stroke) but 4.120" is factory specification.

The Pontiac 215 can be identified by looking at the driver's side of the block. In the lower right area are raised letters spelling out Pontiac.

L6 Casting Numbers Chart

Block identification numbers are located about midway on the passenger side of the block. These can be found almost directly below the first retaining bolt on the back side cover.

Chevrolet Passenger Cars

194 CID/3.1L

Year	Block	Crank	Head
1962-'67	3782856	3788424	3788380
	3833057	3820618	3788414
			3824435
			3874883

230 CID/3.6L

Year	Block	Crank	Head
1963-'65	3788406	as above	3824437
			3864886
			3872708
			3872710
1966-'70	3850817	3850817	3824437
	3854036	3854036	3864886
	3877178	3877178	3872708
	3921968	3921968	3885052

250 CID/4.1L without integral intake manifold

Year	Block	Crank	Head
1966-'79	328575	460407	331184
	348675	2779954	3824437
	358825	3876802	3864886
	366855		3872708
	377127		3885052
	473483		3895052
	2775308		3927763
	3850817	3962084	6259693
	3854036		
	3877178		
	93403466		

Chevrolet and GMC Trucks

250 CID/4.1L without integral intake manifold

Year	Block	Crank	Head
1962-'79	328575	460407	3895052
	348675	2779954	3927763
	366855	3876802	3962084
	377127		
	2775308		
	3850817		
	3854036		
	3877178		
	3921968		

292 CID/4.8L without integral intake manifold

Year	Block	Crank	Head
1963-'66	3789404	3789412	3799019
	3851659		3824437
	3921970	forged 6 counter	3864890
	3994258	weights–7/16" bolt	
		holes on flange	
		3855914N	
		3886061N	
		cast 6 counter	
		weights–7/16" bolt	
		holes on flange	
1967-'90	328578	0363	329609
	352194	3884653	331182
	377129	3910362	3799019
	3789404		3824437
	3851659	cast 12 counter	3864890
	3921970	weights–1/2" bolt	3864980
	3994258	holes on flange	3895052
	14002009		3927763
	93403467		3962086
	93406004		86411148
			93400104
			93413990

Crank casting number location.

Crank forging number location.

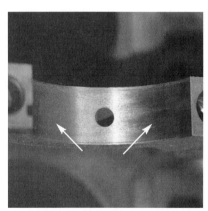

Look at main bearing bores for signs of wear (may indicate need for align hone).

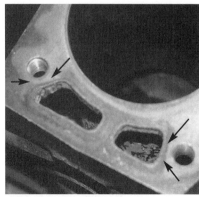

Rear deck weak areas adjacent to water passages.

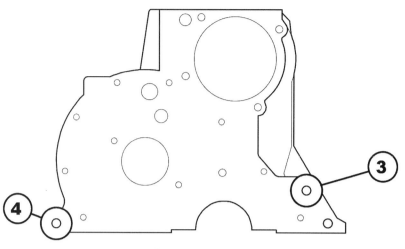

194 Cu. In. BLOCK

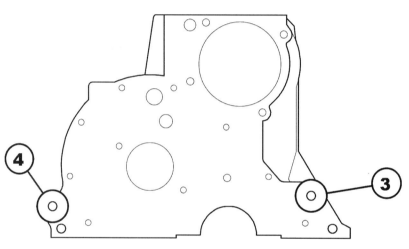

1963 thru 1966 230/250 Cu. In. & 1973 up BLOCKS

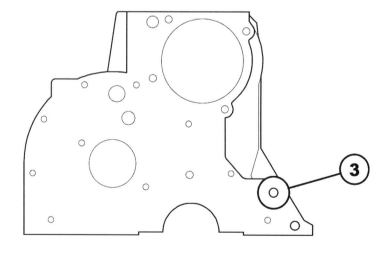

1967 - 1972 250 Cu. In. BLOCK

STD-LD FRONT
ACCESSORY MOUNT CHANGES

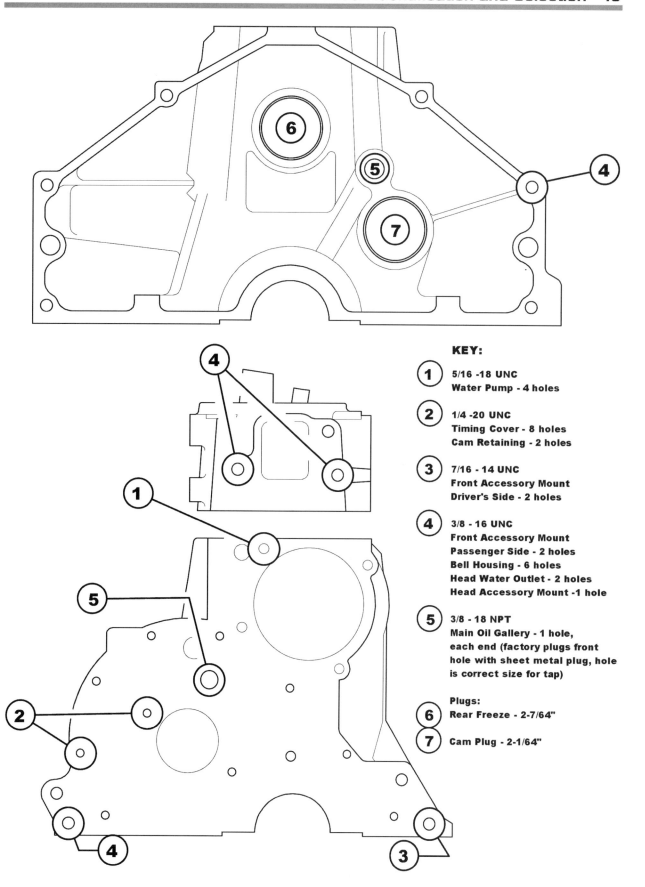

KEY:

1 5/16 -18 UNC
Water Pump - 4 holes

2 1/4 -20 UNC
Timing Cover - 8 holes
Cam Retaining - 2 holes

3 7/16 - 14 UNC
Front Accessory Mount
Driver's Side - 2 holes

4 3/8 - 16 UNC
Front Accessory Mount
Passenger Side - 2 holes
Bell Housing - 6 holes
Head Water Outlet - 2 holes
Head Accessory Mount -1 hole

5 3/8 - 18 NPT
Main Oil Gallery - 1 hole,
each end (factory plugs front
hole with sheet metal plug, hole
is correct size for tap)

Plugs:
6 Rear Freeze - 2-7/64"

7 Cam Plug - 2-1/64"

STD-LD Hole Schedule Front & Rear

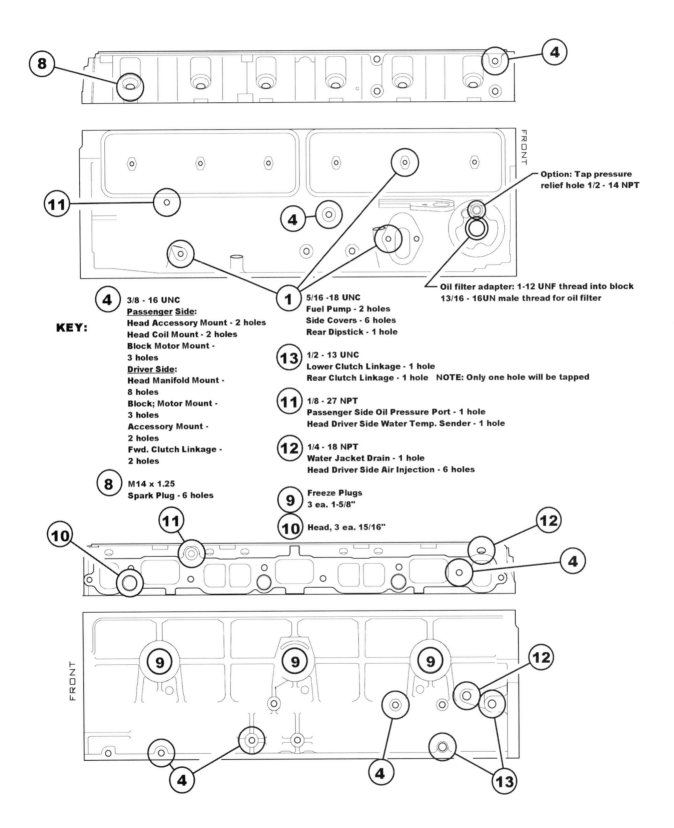

Option: Tap pressure relief hole 1/2 - 14 NPT

Oil filter adapter: 1-12 UNF thread into block 13/16 - 16UN male thread for oil filter

KEY:

4 3/8 - 16 UNC
Passenger Side:
Head Accessory Mount - 2 holes
Head Coil Mount - 2 holes
Block Motor Mount -
3 holes
Driver Side:
Head Manifold Mount -
8 holes
Block; Motor Mount -
3 holes
Accessory Mount -
2 holes
Fwd. Clutch Linkage -
2 holes

8 M14 x 1.25
Spark Plug - 6 holes

1 5/16 -18 UNC
Fuel Pump - 2 holes
Side Covers - 6 holes
Rear Dipstick - 1 hole

13 1/2 - 13 UNC
Lower Clutch Linkage - 1 hole
Rear Clutch Linkage - 1 hole   NOTE: Only one hole will be tapped

11 1/8 - 27 NPT
Passenger Side Oil Pressure Port - 1 hole
Head Driver Side Water Temp. Sender - 1 hole

12 1/4 - 18 NPT
Water Jacket Drain - 1 hole
Head Driver Side Air Injection - 6 holes

9 Freeze Plugs
3 ea. 1-5/8"

10 Head, 3 ea. 15/16"

STD-LD BLOCK & HEAD

STD-LD DIPSTICK LOCATIONS

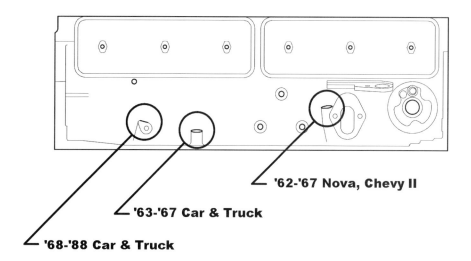

'62-'67 Nova, Chevy II

'63-'67 Car & Truck

'68-'88 Car & Truck

STD-LD CLUTCH PEDAL LINKAGE MOUNTINGS

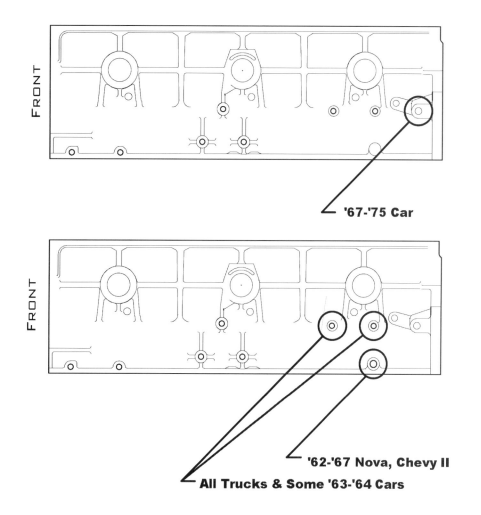

FRONT

'67-'75 Car

FRONT

'62-'67 Nova, Chevy II

All Trucks & Some '63-'64 Cars

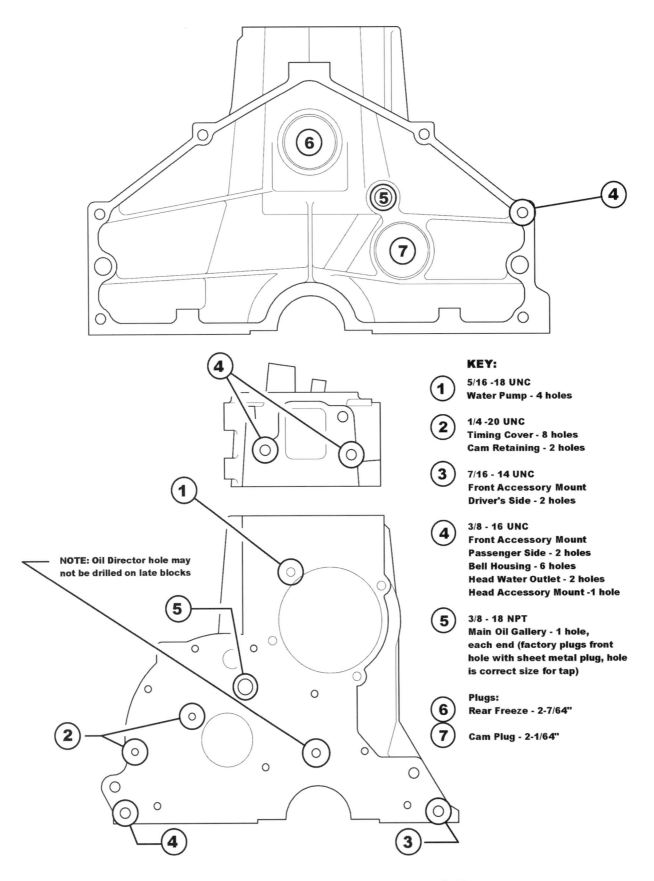

KEY:

1 5/16 -18 UNC
Water Pump - 4 holes

2 1/4 -20 UNC
Timing Cover - 8 holes
Cam Retaining - 2 holes

3 7/16 - 14 UNC
Front Accessory Mount
Driver's Side - 2 holes

4 3/8 - 16 UNC
Front Accessory Mount
Passenger Side - 2 holes
Bell Housing - 6 holes
Head Water Outlet - 2 holes
Head Accessory Mount -1 hole

5 3/8 - 18 NPT
Main Oil Gallery - 1 hole,
each end (factory plugs front
hole with sheet metal plug, hole
is correct size for tap)

Plugs:
6 Rear Freeze - 2-7/64"

7 Cam Plug - 2-1/64"

NOTE: Oil Director hole may
not be drilled on late blocks

HD-TD Hole Schedule - Front & Rear

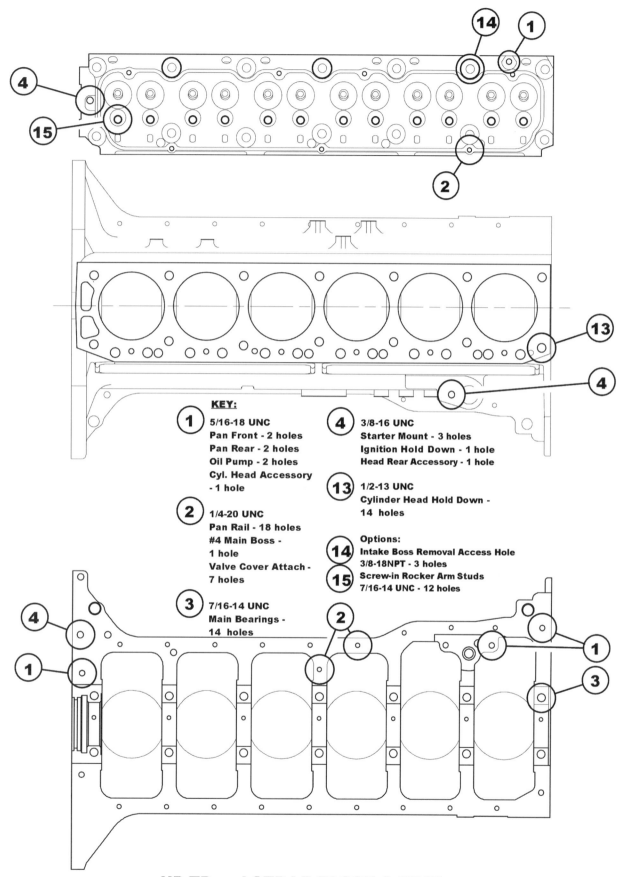

KEY:

1 5/16-18 UNC
Pan Front - 2 holes
Pan Rear - 2 holes
Oil Pump - 2 holes
Cyl. Head Accessory
- 1 hole

2 1/4-20 UNC
Pan Rail - 18 holes
#4 Main Boss -
1 hole
Valve Cover Attach -
7 holes

3 7/16-14 UNC
Main Bearings -
14 holes

4 3/8-16 UNC
Starter Mount - 3 holes
Ignition Hold Down - 1 hole
Head Rear Accessory - 1 hole

13 1/2-13 UNC
Cylinder Head Hold Down -
14 holes

Options:
14 Intake Boss Removal Access Hole
3/8-18NPT - 3 holes
15 Screw-in Rocker Arm Studs
7/16-14 UNC - 12 holes

HD-TD and STD-LD BLOCK & HEAD

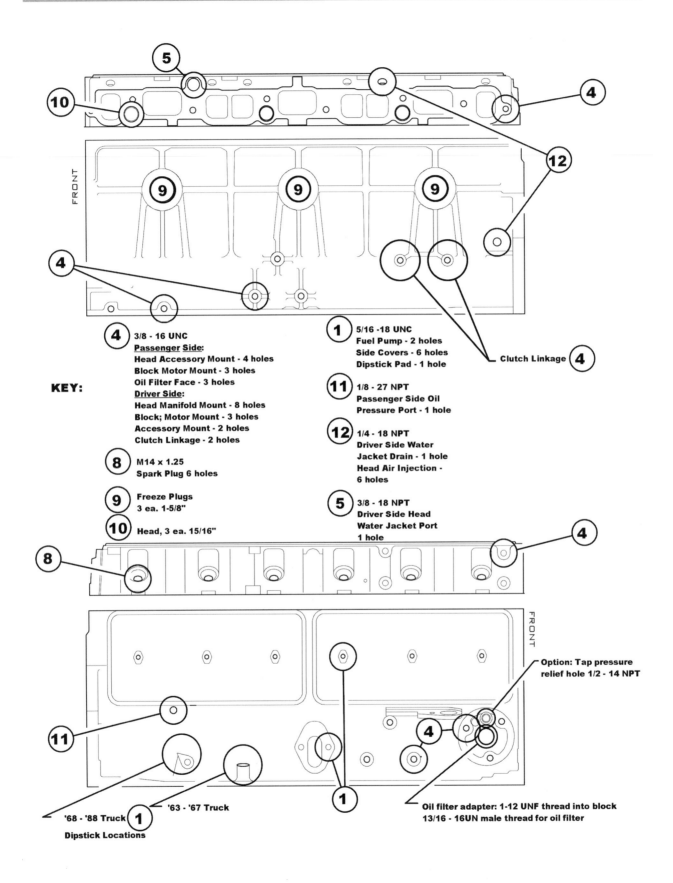

KEY:

4 3/8 - 16 UNC
Passenger Side:
Head Accessory Mount - 4 holes
Block Motor Mount - 3 holes
Oil Filter Face - 3 holes
Driver Side:
Head Manifold Mount - 8 holes
Block; Motor Mount - 3 holes
Accessory Mount - 2 holes
Clutch Linkage - 2 holes

8 M14 x 1.25
Spark Plug 6 holes

9 Freeze Plugs
3 ea. 1-5/8"

10 Head, 3 ea. 15/16"

1 5/16 -18 UNC
Fuel Pump - 2 holes
Side Covers - 6 holes
Dipstick Pad - 1 hole

11 1/8 - 27 NPT
Passenger Side Oil
Pressure Port - 1 hole

12 1/4 - 18 NPT
Driver Side Water
Jacket Drain - 1 hole
Head Air Injection -
6 holes

5 3/8 - 18 NPT
Driver Side Head
Water Jacket Port
1 hole

Clutch Linkage **4**

Option: Tap pressure
relief hole 1/2 - 14 NPT

Oil filter adapter: 1-12 UNF thread into block
13/16 - 16UN male thread for oil filter

'63 - '67 Truck

'68 - '88 Truck **1**

Dipstick Locations

HD-TD BLOCK & HEAD

HD-TD DIPSTICK LOCATIONS

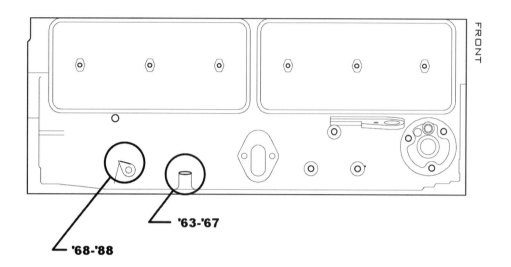

'63-'67

'68-'88

HD-TD CLUTCH PEDAL LINKAGE MOUNTING

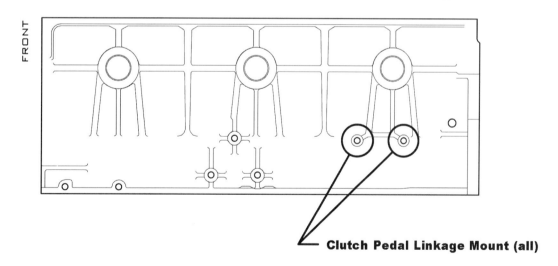

Clutch Pedal Linkage Mount (all)

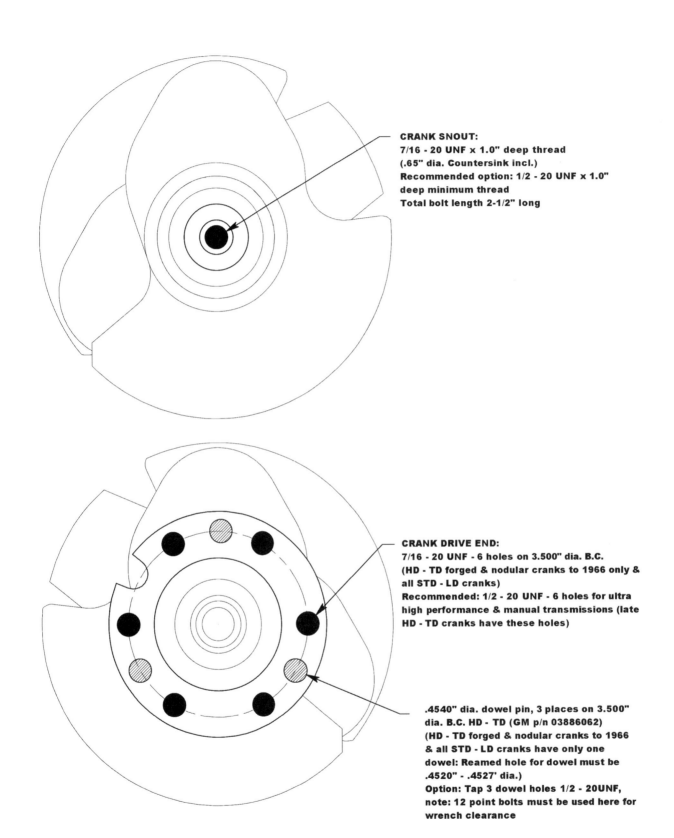

CRANK SNOUT:
7/16 - 20 UNF x 1.0" deep thread
(.65" dia. Countersink incl.)
Recommended option: 1/2 - 20 UNF x 1.0"
deep minimum thread
Total bolt length 2-1/2" long

CRANK DRIVE END:
7/16 - 20 UNF - 6 holes on 3.500" dia. B.C.
(HD - TD forged & nodular cranks to 1966 only &
all STD - LD cranks)
Recommended: 1/2 - 20 UNF - 6 holes for ultra
high performance & manual transmissions (late
HD - TD cranks have these holes)

.4540" dia. dowel pin, 3 places on 3.500"
dia. B.C. HD - TD (GM p/n 03886062)
(HD - TD forged & nodular cranks to 1966
& all STD - LD cranks have only one
dowel: Reamed hole for dowel must be
.4520" - .4527' dia.)
Option: Tap 3 dowel holes 1/2 - 20UNF,
note: 12 point bolts must be used here for
wrench clearance

HD - TD and STD - LD CRANKSHAFT HOLE SCHEDULE

Chapter 4

Machining Operations

- Preparing the selected block for all of the machining operations needed to transform it from mild to wild

The Chevy six block is a sound design capable of supporting hundreds more horsepower than it does in stock use. This happy fact works in our favor when preparing these blocks for enthusiast use. Of course, some Chevy six blocks are better suited to hot rodding than others, and all benefit from careful machine shop attention.

Preliminary Work

The block should be subjected to the following operations after it passes the initial inspection procedures:

1. Deburr of excess casting flash.
2. Enlarge pushrod pathways for high lift cam travel—when running cam lifts over .600" and/or 3/8" pushrods.
3. Clean and inspect main bearing bolts.
4. Drill block to accept V8 heavy duty offset mounted starter when fitting for large diameter flywheel or flexplate (168 tooth)—1973 and later blocks are drilled for both flywheels. Note: if you plan to use a mini-gear reduction starter, this step is unnecessary.
5. If dipstick is not to be used, remove tube and tap for 1/8" pipe plug; no drilling is

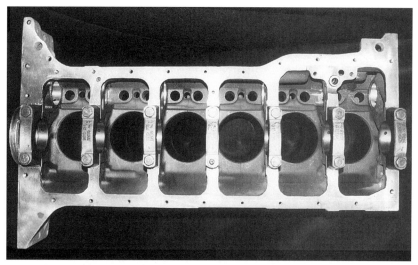

Look for excess casting flash throughout the bottom end, particularly on the cam side of the block. There is a lot of variation in quality—from near perfect as cast (shown here) to excess flashing and even casting sand still present in nooks and crannies.

Beneath oil pump is another prime area to find flashing.

necessary, the factory hole is the correct size for the tap. Be sure to Loctite® plug in place for secure seal.
6. Chase all threaded holes.
7. Clean main oil gallery with stainless brush.
8. Replace cam bearings if necessary.

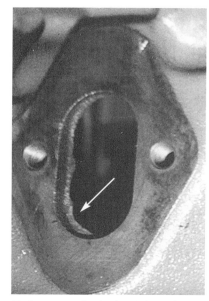

Fuel pump opening is almost always in need of deburring.

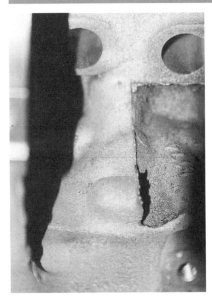

Passenger side of the block along cam journals beneath lifter gallery.

Example of sand from casting process present.

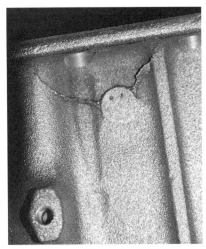

Front side cover (lifter gallery) flashing.

9. Replace core (freeze) plugs.
10. Replace main oil gallery plugs (tap the front opening for screw-in type if not already equipped.) Be sure to use a shallow plug so it doesn't interfere with the number one cam bearing oil feed.
11. Deburr and smooth the oil entry hole from the oil pump and smooth around central return boss. Replace the oil filter bypass valve GM #5575416 or tap and plug to assure full-filtered oil flow. A very low restriction filter should be used for racing such as a System 1®, with stainless screen and removable cap for easy inspection. Part #312361 BP works well. This is the Chevy V8 spin-on. When faced with space limitations, a remote filter, either single or dual, can be used. For street, use the standard high quality spin-on, or, if room permits, a 2-quart low restriction truck filter is available.

Boring

Stock bore for the HD-TD is 3.875". The relationship between bore and cubic inches of displacement is approximately 4.5 cu. in. per .030" of overbore. This is based on a stock stroke of 4.120". The relationship between bore and cubic inches is approximately 4.0 cubic inches of displacement per .030" of overbore on the 250 CID engine and 3.5 cubic inches of displacement per .030" of

Displacement Charts

194 at stock stroke (3.250")

Overbore	.030	.060	.080	.090	.100	.125
Bore Size	3.593	3.623	3.643	3.653	3.663	3.688
CID	198	201	203	204	205	208

215 (Pontiac) at stock stroke (3.250")

Overbore	.030	.060	.080	.090	.100	.125
Bore Size	3.780	3.810	3.830	3.840	3.850	3.875
CID	219	222	225	226	227	230

230 at stock stroke (3.250")

Overbore	.030	.060	.080	.090	.100	.125
Bore Size	3.905	3.935	3.955	3.965	3.975	4.000
CID	234	237	240	241	242	245

250 at stock stroke (3.530")

Overbore	.030	.060	.080	.090	.100	.125
Bore Size	3.905	3.935	3.955	3.965	3.975	4.00
CID	254	258	260	262	263	266

292 at stock stroke (4.120")

Overbore	.030	.060	.080	.090	.100	.125
Bore Size	3.905	3.935	3.955	3.965	3.975	4.000
CID	296	301	304	306	307	311

overbore on both the 194 and 230 CID engines based on a stock stroke as noted in the chart.

As you bore the cylinders larger, the walls become thinner, which means that at some point a trade-off occurs. That is, whatever is gained in the form of displacement, you lose when the cylinder walls flex under load and the piston rings cannot maintain adequate seal. Sleeving the block, although expensive, bypasses this problem but runs head-long into deck instability and potential head gasket problems. Additionally, we have to provide for proportional increases in air flow through an already limited cylinder head design. The bore size should, therefore, be held as close to standard as possible (especially for endurance racing, with +.060" (3.935") considered the practical limit with non-hybrid head and normal water passage retention.

Water Jacket Filling—Blocks used for short duration events (with maximum head rework) may receive up to a 4.000" bore when water passages are filled with Hard Blok® to within 1-1/2 inch of the deck surface, using water only in the head and the top of the block circulated by an external pump. Glen Self goes one step further to stabilize the cylinder walls. He partially bores the wall to create a dry wall with a step at the bottom and then uses a chromoly thin sleeve pressed in place. This method forms a very strong straight and round cylinder that does not destabilize the deck surface of the block.

Sonic check—A sonic check of the cylinder wall thickness on the HD-TD is mandatory when boring anything beyond .080" oversize. On the STD-LD series blocks, check on anything over .100". If you contemplate

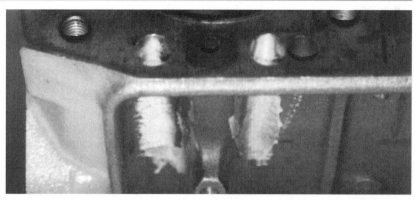

Block relieved for pushrod clearance. High lift cams and/or 3/8" pushrods require this.

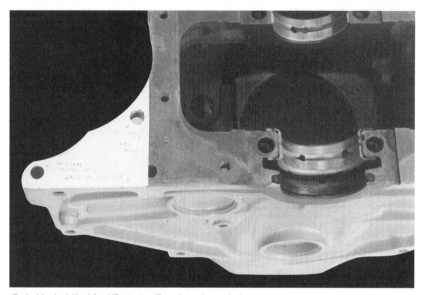

Early block drilled for HD starter. Template shown below.

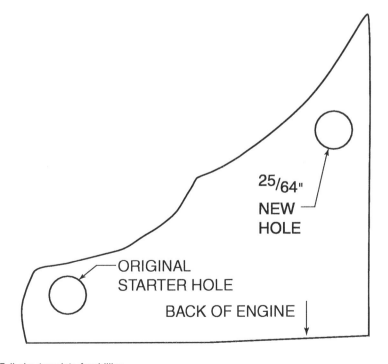

Full-size template for drilling.

Tap dipstick hole for plug—full competition only (1/8" pipe).

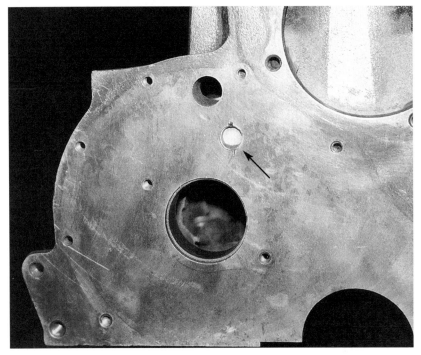

Some blocks have sheet metal plugs staked in (arrow)—remove and tap for shallow pipe plug (3/8"–18 NPT). Be sure not to go so deep as to block front cam bearing lube hole.

chambers. When honing with this type of plate you must hone from the bottom of the block. This procedure is more difficult and requires more set up time than a conventional torque plate. For this reason, a conventional torque plate is preferred. No matter which torque-plate is used, always remember to torque the main bearing caps before honing begins.

Although using a torque plate seems like a lot of extra work, do not underestimate the value of a properly sealed and round cylinder!

Bore Finish—Bore finish should approximate that achieved with 400 grit stones (smooth) and finished with a plateau brush. If the cylinder walls are left too rough, piston and ring life will be adversely affected. Conversely, if the walls are left too smooth, the piston rings may not seat and the cylinder will not hold pressure. Always check with the ring manufacturer for the correct finish for your application.

Rod Clearances

Remember to grind the bottom of the cylinders and oil pan rails for connecting rod clearance, if needed, when using aluminum rods. See the section on rods for detailed information. Clean cylinder wall with 556™ spray and white paper towels after final work and before assembly.

Deck Surface

The block and cylinder head surfaces must be true to obtain proper head gasket seal. Maximum decking recommended is .030".

O-Rings

When contemplating compression ratios above 10.5

filling the block, do so first, and allow full curing before boring and honing.

Torque Plate—All honing for a competition engine should be done with a torque plate installed. For street use this is strictly an option. Use a head gasket of the same type as will be used in the final engine assembly (Fel-Pro® Part #8006 P.T. or 1025 HP is recommended). If your cylinders have been O-ringed,

O-ring wire should be in place and all head bolts should be coated with sealer and torqued in the same sequence and to the same final torque as the cylinder head itself will be. Don't forget the head bolt washers! If a stud kit is to replace stock head bolts, be sure these are used with the torque-plate.

A torque plate may be made from an old cylinder head by milling out the combustion to 1, it is preferable to O-ring the cylinders due to the wide head bolt spacing of this engine. O-ringing eliminates the need for either a special steel shim head gasket, which is no longer available commercially, or the replacement of head bolts with studs.

O-ring groove should be cut to about .030" depth. Soft copper wire may be obtained from an electrical supply house. A diameter of .036" is available in multi-strand #6Aw6 600V Type THHV wire and is used by separating into single strands of about 27" each. Some racers prefer stainless wire in high compression (14.5 to 1 and above) or supercharged/ turbocharged applications. Here you want to create maximum resistance to blow out, so we cut a .025" groove and use a .041" wire. The difference between the depth of the block groove and the diameter of the wire creates a solid compression seal. Each ring is cut diagonally and rolled into place (do not hammer) with the opposing end cut to a complementary angle thereby forming a no-gap butt placed adjacent to one of the head bolts (or studs) for maximum clamping effect.

Some racers prefer to O-ring the head instead of the block, which also produces satisfactory results. Fel-Pro® has a high performance head gasket, Part #1025, with O-rings around each cylinder. This gasket all but eliminates the need to O-ring the deck or head when used with a stud kit.

Lower End

The inherent strength of this seven-main bearing design does not require special girdles or studs for the bearing caps, even for quite high horsepower engines (350 HP or less). Factory

Variations of Oil Filter Pad

HD-TD and some truck STD-LDs. The three holes are for a 90° filter adapter. See page 4.

STD-LD.

STD-LD.

STD-LD.

tolerances are very accurate and align honing is rarely needed.

In order to check, install new main bearings, lubricate and place the crankshaft into the main bearing saddles and torque the main caps to specifications. Crankshaft should spin freely and bearing clearances should measure between .0010" and .0025".

The main bearing caps are cast with an arrow, which points towards the front of the block. The oil pick-up tube extension brace attaches to the #5 main

Tap for full flow oil filtration (1/2"–14NPT) only full competition engines. Note full smoothing and additional oil pump exit hole in this oval track STD-LD block. Note full polishing of the lifter galley—meticulous attention to detail.

Smooth and deburr oil entry and exit holes.

Stock oil filter adapter left and center with System 1® sleeve in place at right.

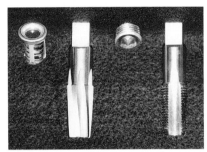

Stock pressure relief valve—ream/tap and plug.

Torque plate mounted on engine for boring and honing.

O-ringed block with V8 bolt pattern for hybrid head.

Marking block for clearance using maximum competition aluminum rods.

Note wear on main bearing saddle (indicative of need for align hone).

Arrow on main bearing cap indicates position toward the front of the block.

Block clearancing shown for maximum competition aluminum rods.

bearing cap (camshaft side of the block). Stock main bearing cap retaining bolts are adequate for most applications. Beyond 550 HP and for all endurance applications, studs become mandatory; at extreme horse-power levels (600 HP), a girdle tying main caps 4, 5 and 6 together is a wise investment.

O-ringed head.

Chapter 5

Oiling System Modifications

- The basic oil path
- Understanding oil system modifications
- Specific thoughts and recommendations

The Chevrolet six cylinder oiling system picks up oil from the pan and directs oil from the pump to the oil filter and then to the main gallery.

This gallery runs lengthwise on the passenger side of the block intersecting the valve lifter bores and feeding main, rod and cam bearings and timing gears at the front of the block. The oil flow is metered upward through the valve lifters following a path up the pushrods to feed the overhead rocker arms.

Oil returning from the cylinder head drains around the pushrod holes and collects behind the side covers along the valve lifter gallery to be drained through holes above the camshaft into the oil pan. The front lifter gallery also provides distributor shaft lubrication and extra drainage to the front timing cover area.

Because both STD-LDs and HD-TDs were used as truck engines, the oiling system, especially to the cylinder head area, provides for sufficient volumes of oil to assure long life. In fact, this stock oiling system is very good as it is and many successful race engines have used it with virtually no modifications. Although there is power to be gained with proper modifications, the gains are not of the

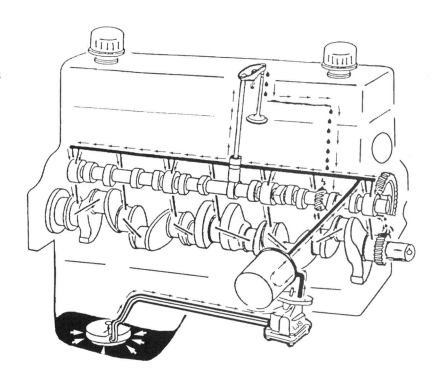

Line drawing showing stock oiling system and the path of oil from the pan to various engine locations and its return.

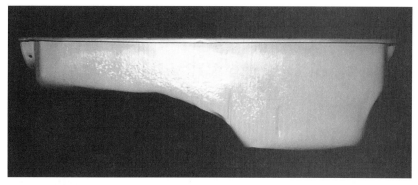

The HD-TD wet sump pan is the most common pan used for competition due to its much deeper front section.

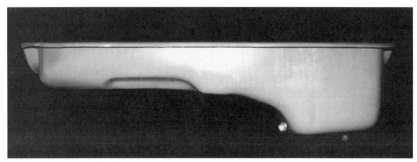

STD-LD standard pan for most passenger and truck applications.

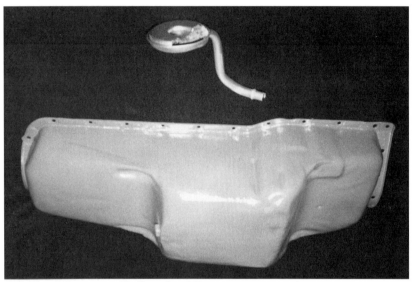

STD-LD variation pan used in Chevy II and Nova passenger cars only.

Modified deep sump Chevy II/Nova pan adds 2-quart additional capacity.

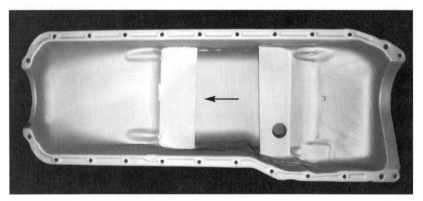

Note anti-surge plate added to pan.

same order of magnitude as those achieved by V8 motors. This is because the cylinders of the inline engines are vertical and it is less likely that oil will be thrown into the cylinders as it flies off the spinning crankshaft.

When modifying the oiling system, we need to keep three goals in mind:

1. Maintain adequate oil volume and pressure to the main and rod bearings—especially those towards the rear of the engine.
2. Reduce internal oil leakage and restrict the volume of oil to the cylinder head.
3. Prevent the returning oil from the cylinder head from falling on the camshaft and being picked up by the rods with consequent "roping" around the crankshaft causing attendant horsepower loss and aeration. This is for racing applications only and may have negative effects on a street driven camshaft.

I will describe three proven systems based on anticipated power production.

System I: Street-strip or oval track up to 275 HP

Standard (low) volume oil pump, stock HD-TD oil pan, special oil restricting valve lifters (GM #5232695—Big block Chevy V8) or custom pushrods with small orifice may be used in lieu of special lifters to achieve the same results, stock rocker arms.

Note: High-volume pump is not recommended due to marginal distributor/oil pump drive gear load capacity.

System II: Drag Strip only up to 400 HP

Standard (low) volume oil pump, deep sump modified oil pan, special oil restricting valve lifters and small orifice pushrods. Edge orifice solid lifters from Sealed Power #AT887 for flat tappet cam, roller rocker arms, oil drain back return holes radiused in lifter gallery.

Note: Do not use stock GM lifters for Z-28 V8 flat tappet cam or V8 roller lifters.

System III: Super Strip up to 600 HP

Standard (low) volume oil pump, deep sump modified oil pan, special oil restricting valve lifters, main lifter gallery tube insertion, roller rocker arms, oil drain back return holes in lifter gallery blocked, pushrod side covers modified for external drain back and oil pan venting (see modification notes).

Modification Notes

Tube insertion—main oil gallery. For high-horsepower engines, track use only, it may be

Modified rear sump with anti-surge plate (note slight angle to front to promote drainage).

Note drainbacks from side covers and additional 4" section to increase pan capacity by two quarts.

Modified rear sump with directional screen in the front pan section and block portion mounted to the last three main bearing caps. Pan is standard 5-quart capacity.

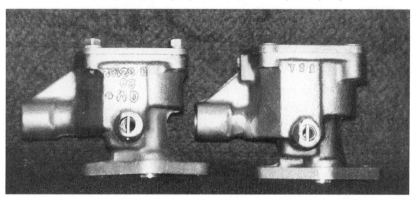

Standard (regular-volume) oil pump vs. heavy-duty (high-volume) oil pump. Note high-volume pump is about 1/4" taller.

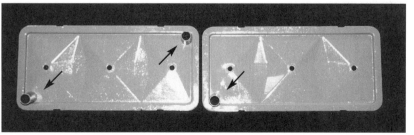

Modified side covers for external drain back and pan ventilation.

Fuel pump block off plate modified for pan ventilation.

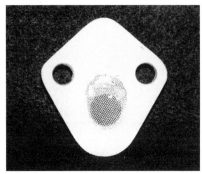

Back side with screen epoxied in place.

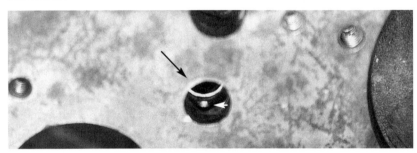

Front block view with main oil gallery tube insertion (black arrow) (plug removed). Note: do not cover the cam bearing feed hole (white arrow).

Lifter bore view with tube insertion. Note .020" oil hole.

Fully prepped STD-LD with reinforcing plate in place of water pump.

desirable to further restrict cylinder head oil flow (in addition to use of special oil restricting lifters) and to enhance main and rod bearing oil supply. This can be accomplished by inserting a mild thin-wall steel tube into the main oil gallery front to back, thereby completely blocking all supply points. Once this is accomplished, the tube must be compressed in order to allow proper clearance for valve lifter insertion. Oil passages are then opened for full main and rod bearing feed; while in the lifter area, feed to the valve lifter is severely restricted by the provision of only a .020" hole. A special hardened punch is used to make this tiny opening.

Tube Alternative—Sleeve each lifter bore with a bronze insert pre-drilled with only a .020" hole exposed to the main gallery. Deburr the inside by drilling a 1/8" hole 180° away. These holes do not have to be plugged as they will be against solid block when the sleeves are pressed in place and aligned with the .020" hole exposed to the main gallery.

Oil Drain Back—Valve lifter gallery. When using Oiling System III, oil that is normally drained by holes in the lifter gallery are blocked, use 3/8" O.D. x 1-1/2" long copper tubing (available from plumbing supply house). These tubes are tapped into place and crimped closed. No sealers are used. The small hole to lubricate the distributor shaft is left open, as well as the opening to the timing gear area.

Side Covers—Lifter gallery. Once the stock oil drain back holes are sealed, provisions must be made for external oil drainage and pan venting. The side covers are therefore drilled in the lower left corner for 3/4" I.D. external drain hose connections. These will attach to the oil pan below the level of the crank and rods and provide a new return path for oil coming from the cylinder head area. This effectively eliminates drain back oil falling on the camshaft and being picked up by the rods.

The back side cover is drilled in the upper right hand corner for pan ventilation connection. This will attach to the fuel pump block off plate.

Block Off Plate—Fuel pump. Many commercially available block off plates are too thin when modified and will result in leakage. Therefore, a plate is made of 1/4" steel, drilled to accept the pan ventilation hose 3/4" I.D. and ground flat.

Oil Director—Timing gears. Oil is fed from the number one camshaft bearing saddle through a block passage terminating between the timing gears under the front timing cover. A small tube fitting presses into this orifice and directs the oil onto the timing gears. This director should be fixed in place with Loctite® Red (stud and bearing retainer). Tip projection points directly towards the driver side number one main bearing retainer bolt. This tube is filled with epoxy or brazed shut and redrilled with only a .030" hole to limit oil flow.

The oil director is eliminated on later model engines—splash oiling has proven sufficient for street use.

Oiling System Components

Oil Pump—No internal modification is necessary, both standard and high-volume pumps perform well for most applications. Choose an appropriate pump based on horsepower and application. Street applications may use the high-volume pump, but many racers feel that the standard pump is best, as the high volume pump only adds

Block view after oil drain hole modifications.

Oil director modified after being filled and redrilled with .030" restrictor hole.

Oil director. Note direction of the tip towards the number one main bearing bolt—driver side.

Front view STD-LD with oil director hole (arrow).

Front view HD-TD late block with no oil director. GM determined splash oiling was sufficient.

External oil pump modification when running aluminum Superods on small forgings.

When using large forging Superods (fueler rods), the body of the pump is cut to allow a straight shot with the reamer and tap to plug the original pump inlet. Note angle of cut started.

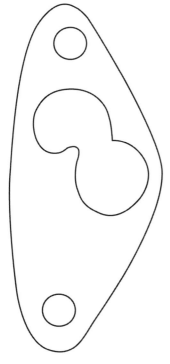

Full-size template for oil pump to block gasket.

Note angle of cut from bottom towards top cut.

Exposed inlet opening for reamer and tap.

Inlet hole tapped and Allen head plug inserted. Be sure to seal in position.

stress to a weak drive design. If the high-volume pump is used, you may wish to increase the oil volume capacity of the pan. To identify a used pump and distinguish between standard and high-volume, measure the height

of the body from mounting flange to the top flat. A 3-1/4" measurement means a standard pump, a 3-1/2" measurement means a high-volume pump. The external pump housing adjacent to pick-up tube must be modified for additional clearance when using aluminum Superods on small forging—HD-TD only. With larger forging or billet rods, the top of the pump must be replaced in order to move the oil pick-up tube out of the way. The original pick-up hole is tapped and plugged.

Oil Pick-up Tube—This tube presses into the oil pump body and is supported by a brace attaching to the #5 main bearing retaining bolt.

Because of this brace, it is not necessary to braze, weld or otherwise fix the pick-up tube into the body of the pump. Once in place, you may wish to seal against potential air leaks by putting a thin layer of epoxy around the joint.

In order to use aluminum rods and obtain the proper clearance, all series engines should use the HD-TD style pick-up tube.

The pick-up tube must be extended when using a deep sump pan. Be sure to allow 3/8" clearance between pan surface and pick-up screen.

Oil Pan—The standard HD-TD pan is a rear sump, five-quart capacity design. It is available from Chevrolet under part #3938923 and comes complete with pick-up tube and #5 main bearing stud and brace.

This pan differs from the STD-LD series engine design in that it has a front portion that is much deeper and consequently helps keep the oil away from the spinning crank assembly. The pan and associated parts are completely inter-changeable with the STD-LD series engine and so are preferred for those engines also, if the chassis can accommodate the larger dimensions.

Under maximum acceleration oil is forced against the back wall of the pan and is driven upward onto the spinning crank assembly. This results in a loss of horsepower as well as a flooding of the rear main bearing seals and oil pan gaskets. To prevent this, a rear baffle is added, tilted at a slight angle for drainage. With the addition of this baffle, the pan can be used as is for street and mild street/strip activities.

Drag Pans—Full competition drag engines need, in addition to the rear baffle, the sump portion enlarged. A four-inch section is added, thereby lowering the oil level in the pan to minimize windage effects from the spinning crankshaft. Oil drain back tubes are added below the surface of the oil for cylinder head drainage.

The interior of the pan is covered with unidirectional mesh, in order to prevent oil thrown from the crank assembly from bouncing off the smooth pan surface and returning to the spinning crankshaft. Maximum horsepower engines may also use a kickout on the passenger side of the pan and/or crankshaft scrapers to keep the oil off the spinning assembly.

Oval Pans—Oval track engines need a special pan made with baffles and left turn sump and pickup such as made by Precision Engine Service.

Custom made aluminum pans are available from several sources; these can be made as wet sumps or dry sumps. Probably the most sophisticated pan work has been done by Glen Self. Self uses a wet sump with full pan kickout (the starter is moved to the driver's side of the block). A three-stage external pump provides oil pressure with one

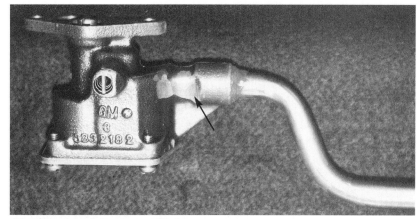
Alternative view of oil pump modification.

A new pump cover with larger pick-up tube is welded to the top—this becomes the new oil inlet.

Be sure to allow .060" clearance between rods and pump.

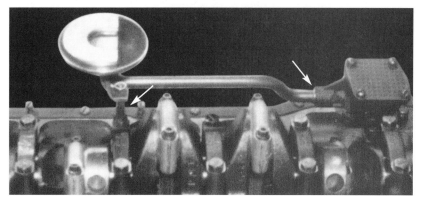
Pick-up for most applications presses into the pump body. The brace for the pick-up tube attaches to the number five main bearing cap.

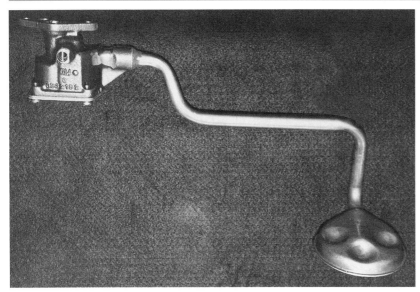

Seal press-in joint with a layer of epoxy or high temperature silicone (stock tube and pick-up shown).

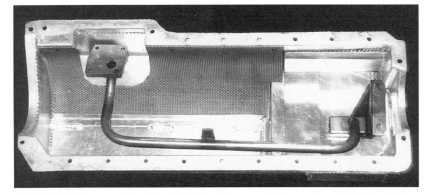

Hamburg aluminum pan showing unidirectional screen and oil pump top with pick-up tube.

stage and creates pan vacuum with the other two stages. This pan design is excellent but is definitely for "ultimate" engines only.

Timing Cover—The only modification to the timing cover is to remove the stock timing tab and fabricate a new one that is compatible with your harmonic balancer selection and positioned where you can readily see and align the timing marks.

It should be noted that the Chevy six does not require a special two-piece timing cover in order to access the camshaft. It is possible to remove the stock timing cover, and hence the camshaft, without removing the oil pan.

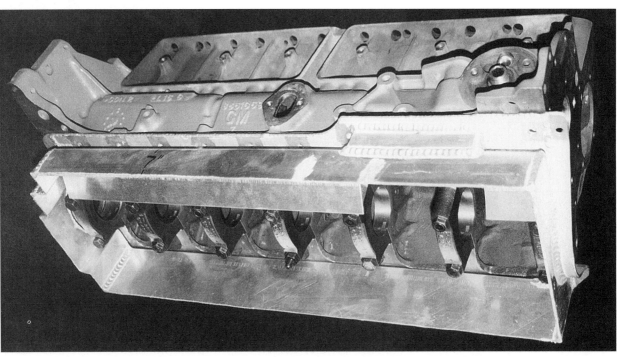

Hamburg aluminum with cut-away sump. Note passenger side kickout. Scraper must be cut to fit crank before use.

Fabricated timing indicator should be easy to view and sharply pointed. This attaches directly under the front cover attachment bolts.

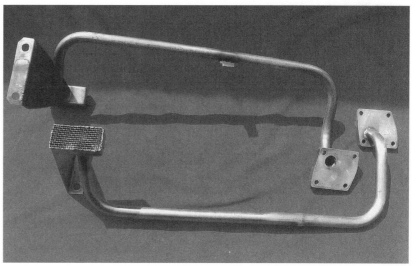

Hamburg oil pump tops and pick-ups shown from above and below.

Wet sump STD-LD oval track engine with belt driven external oil pump.

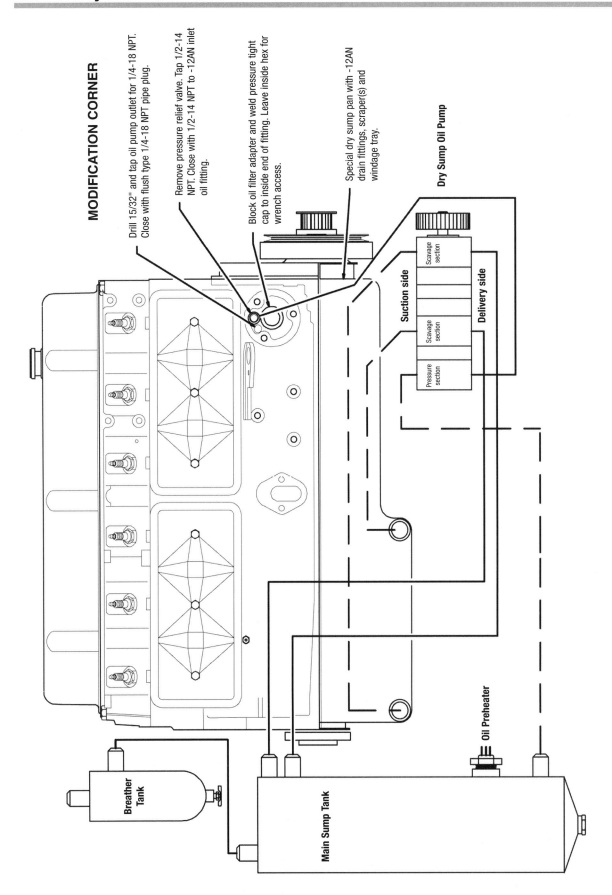

MODIFICATION CORNER

Drill 15/32" and tap oil pump outlet for 1/4-18 NPT. Close with flush type 1/4-18 NPT pipe plug.

Remove pressure relief valve. Tap 1/2-14 NPT. Close with 1/2-14 NPT to -12AN inlet oil fitting.

Block oil filter adapter and weld pressure tight cap to inside end of fitting. Leave inside hex for wrench access.

Special dry sump pan with -12AN drain fittings, scraper(s) and windage tray.

Dry Sump Oil Pump

Scavage section

Suction side

Scavage section

Delivery side

Pressure section

Oil Preheater

Breather Tank

Main Sump Tank

Dry sump oil system layout

Chapter 6

Crankshaft and Timing Gears

- Crank selection and preparation
- Timing gear choices
- How to assemble timing gears to cam and crankshaft
- Torsional dampers and timing marks

Crank Selection

In full-race applications, the Achilles heel of the HD-TD used to be the crankshaft. The combination of a 4.120" stroke and a total length of over 31" and a weight of 73 lbs. could lead to torsional vibration problems not shared by the STD-LD engine series. For these reasons, many racers avoided the HD-TDs and gave up 40+ cubic inches to increase engine longevity. Now, with the advent of excellent harmonic balancers and a careful blending of associated parts, along with proper balancing techniques, there is no need to avoid the HD-TDs because of longevity fears.

Ideally, the HD-TDs should have had a lightweight, fully counterweighted forged steel crankshaft. Unfortunately, Chevrolet never released this important ingredient. Instead, we have basically three crankshafts to consider:

1. 1963—Forged steel shaft not fully counterweighted and only made this one year in the US (these are becoming hard to locate). It was made in Canada through 1964. Six counterweights are found on this shaft. This crankshaft can have additional counterweights added but the

1963 forged steel crankshaft—made only one year. Note six counterweights.

Nodular cast, six-counterweight crank—made 1964–1966 only. Note width of casting line on the shoulder of the number two rod journal compared with the ground-off wide face of the parting line of the forged crankshaft.

The most common crankshaft—12 counterweights, cast. An excellent and reliable choice due to the better balance obtained with the extra counterweights.

43

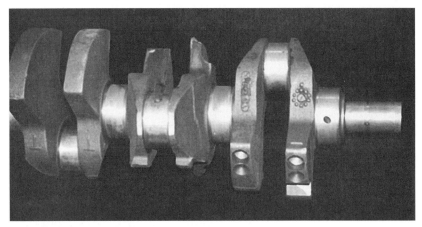

Crankshaft before deburring.

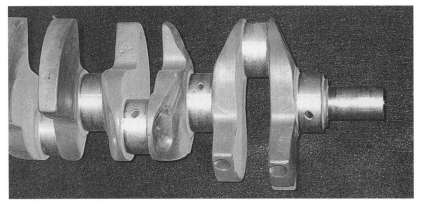

Crankshaft after deburring.

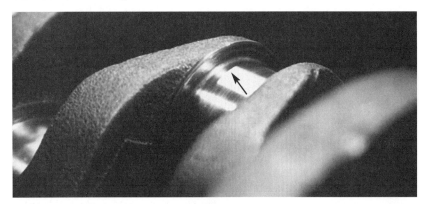

Proper fillet obtained with grinding and polishing.

Oil feed hole—chamfered and polished. Do NOT cross drill a crankshaft—it reduces oil supply at the bearing.

much higher additional expense is hard to justify in terms of added reliability. Forging number: 3789412.

2. 1964–66—Six counterweight nodular cast iron shaft. This crank is lighter and, from an engineering point of view, may be stronger in resisting bending and torsional stresses than the forged steel shaft. This is due to the wide crank arms of this shaft. Therefore, this crankshaft may be the sleeper of the choices available, especially if lightened and combined with very lightweight related components. Casting numbers: 3855914N and 3886061N.

3. 1967 and up—Fully counter-weighted nodular cast iron shaft. This crankshaft is the most commonly used and is readily available both new and used. There are twelve counterweights found on this shaft. Casting numbers: 0363, 3884653, 3910362, 3910363.

Crankshaft Prep

All crankshafts can be used successfully by a careful blending of the right combination of related parts (rods, pistons and harmonic balancer). Always perform a careful visual and magnaflux inspection of any crankshaft before machine work begins (even new crankshafts can occasionally have flaws). Once the integrity of the shaft is assured, perform the following operations:

Deburr—Deburr excess casting flash and file all sharp edges smooth.

Journals—Regrind main and rod journals up to .030" undersize to obtain the largest fillet radius—if necessary. Proper fillet radius must be obtained. Once the radius is obtained, polish the fillet to further reduce

Fully polished STD-LD crank. Note knife edging of counterweights and overall weight reduction of approximately 18 pounds.

the possibility of vibration cracks. Be sure the rod journals are indexed for the exact stroke desired for all racing applications.

Oil Holes—Chamfer oil feed holes. They must be rounded smooth and polished. Extending oil feed holes, an accepted V8 practice, is unnecessary on the HD-TD, although may be helpful for high winding six STD-LD blocks that run in the 7,000 to 9,000 RPM range.

Oil Seal—Always check the crankshaft oil seal mating surfaces and remove nicks with crocus cloth.

Snout—Drill and tap snout of crank for 1/2" x 20NF x 2-1/2" harmonic balancer retainer bolt.

Flange—Chase flywheel/flex plate retaining bolt holes. Replace pilot bushing, if manual transmission is to be used. Remember to have the crankshaft flange faced perpendicular to the centerline. For serious competition use, a roller bearing replacement GM #14061685 or Moroso equivalent is preferred. Be sure dowel pin(s) are in place (early cranks have only one, you may wish to add two more as some late model cranks have). These help keep the flywheel in place. Some racers drill out the dowels and add additional bolts (for a total of 9). These are also 1/2" and require a special 12-point head in order to clear the adjacent bolts. If you are running a forged crank with 7/16" flange bolts, you should drill and tap for 1/2" bolts and

Fully polished STD-LD crank. Note oil hole treatment.

Oil seal mating surface before polishing.

Oil seal mating surface after polishing.

Drill and tap crank snout for 1/2" x 20NF x 2-1/2".

Roller ppilot bearing for maximum competition clutch transmission applications.

Crank flange late 1/2" bolts with dowel pins and stock type pilot bushing in place.

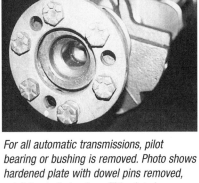

For all automatic transmissions, pilot bearing or bushing is removed. Photo shows hardened plate with dowel pins removed, retaining bolts in place. This plate is unnecessary for most applications.

Aluminum flywheel with pins and hardened plate attached. Flywheel bolts must be torqued to 110 pounds with Loctite® red. Note plate covers dowel pins so they are positively retained.

Side view of plate with retaining bolts.

Crank flange early 7/16" bolts. Note poor condition of flange.

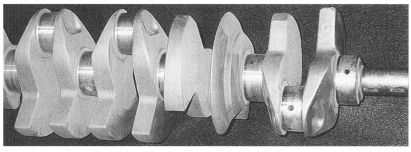

Lightened crankshaft HD-TD.

Straight cut (14° tooth angle) cam and crank gear set. All truck applications—HD-TD—used aluminum cam gear and steel crank gear. Never use the fiber passenger car cam gear for any performance application.

STD-LD fiber cam gear. Do not use.

add the extra bolts at this time.

In my experience in drag racing, I have found that dowel pins and/or additional bolts are not needed when using a flex plate for an automatic transmission. The proper bolts are GM 1/2" #3910367 for flywheels and #19893910368 for flex plates. The proper dowel pins are GM #3886062. These are line reamed in place to keep the flywheel from moving.

Lightening—The HD-TD crankshaft may be lightened as much as 20 lbs. For full competition engines knife-edging and polishing of the counterweights may also be done at this time. The STD-LD series crankshaft can also have a proportional amount of weight removed.

Balance—The crankshaft is balanced very precisely to "0" after all machining operations are complete. Caution: Never groove, chrome or cross-drill the crankshaft!

Timing Gears

Both the STD-LD and the HD-TD utilize a gear drive setup consisting of a cast iron crankshaft gear and an aluminum camshaft gear. This provides what Iskenderian used to refer to as "Immaculate timing"—no timing chain stretch here! Just think, V8 owners have to pay extra for this type of setup!

Gear Selection

Two gear sets were used:

1. A straight cut version (14-degree tooth angle) used on early HD-TDs up until 1966 and all STD-LD block series engines.

2. A heavy-duty pointed tooth version (20-degree tooth angle) used on all later (post-1966) HD-TDs.

These factory gear sets have adequate strength for 99 percent of all applications. Extreme drag engines using very high valve spring pressure (300 lbs. on the seat) and certain endurance oval track applications may want to use a steel camshaft gear. A steel straight cut gear set for the Pontiac Iron Duke competition engine is available from Cloyes, and may be used on our six cylinder Chevy engines.

A steel crank gear is available with three keyway slots for standard, advanced or retarded cam timing. Offset keys are also available to advance or retard the cam with a standard gear.

If you manage to locate a forged crankshaft (made only in 1963), you will need the heavy-duty truck 250 aluminum gear in order to match the crank gear and provide the proper timing.

When running an STD-LD series engine, always use the

HD pointed tooth gear set (20° tooth angle) cam and crank set.

Steel straight cut gear set from Precision Engine Service.

Offset crank woodruff key can be obtained in 2° and 4° intervals (same as small-block Chevy V8—short style).

Spacer (countersunk side up for viewing only) and thrust plate.

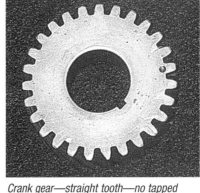

Crank gear—straight tooth—no tapped holes for removal. Here we use a jaws-type puller.

Front of cam and gear drilled for retention with 1/4" x 20NF x 1"—half in the cam and half in the gear.

Timing gear drilled for 1/4" x 20NF x 1" (goes with cam shown at left).

Front of cam drilled for 7/16" x 20NF x 1-1/2" Allen head bolt and washer. The female head of the bolt (socket) can also be used as a 3/8" drive point for a Hilborn fuel injection pump mounted to the front cover.

Glen Self modified stock HD-TD harmonic balancer.

Modified crank gear countersunk versus stock crank gear. Straight cut (14° tooth angle).

Crank gear shown with puller attached to remove the gear.

HD 250 aluminum camshaft gear—never use the pressed fiber gear commonly supplied.

Discontinued GM part numbers may still be available.

Check with any GM dealer to have them run an availability search.

A billet set of crank and cam gears is available from Fontana Automotive. The crank gear has multiple settings for timing choice. This is an excellent set, but expect to spend serious dollars.

Assembly

Crank Gear—It is best to install this after the crankshaft is in the block and torqued in place. The woodruff keys must both be in place. Preheat an oven to 500F. Then put the gear into the oven for 15 minutes. Remove with protective gloves, align with woodruff keys—make sure the timing mark is facing towards the front (towards you, start by hand then drive all the way on using a leftover piece of exhaust tubing (4" x 1-1/2" O.D.). It is best to have your tools laid out and ready so that this process occurs before the gear cools down.

Camshaft Gear—To assemble this gear requires some planning ahead. Place the camshaft into a freezer overnight. You will need a friend to hold the cam once it comes out of the freezer. Preheat an oven to 500F (keep the camshaft in the freezer until the gear is ready). Place the gear into the oven for 15–20 minutes. While waiting for the gear, lay out the spacer ring and thrust plate. It should be noted that the 216-261 Chevy 6 and GMC early engines thrust plates look the same. Beware—these early plates are a different thickness and should not be used. Just before you're ready to remove the gear from the oven, have someone remove the cam from the freezer (use gloves!), stand the cam on the rear bearing, place the spacer ring on (countersunk side goes on first) over the front of the camshaft, then the thrust plate and install the woodruff key in the keyway. Quickly remove the cam timing gear from the oven using insulated gloves. Drop the gear over the front of the camshaft, making sure the keyway groove in the gear is aligned with the woodruff key and the timing mark (0) is facing forward (towards you). Make sure the gear is all the way down against the spacer ring. The thrust plate should be free to move and have slight end play.

Do not use a hammer to install—when it is done correctly the gear will go into place easily. When the gear cools, it will be held in position positively.

Gear Retention

Although some camshaft manufacturers used to provide for a snap ring or bolt retention of the cam gear, this is not necessary when the gear is installed as above and sized to specs for most applications. However, always follow the manufacturer's instructions to avoid potential warranty problems.

Many racers, particularly oval track enthusiasts, install a 1/4" x 20 set screw axially, half in the cam gear and half in the camshaft and Loctite® this in place for added safety. The reason they do this is because of the higher temperatures the engine achieves in oval track applications. I have not found this necessary for street or strip applications. For full competition engines, the cam can be drilled and tapped for a central retaining bolt and washer and the timing cover modified to clear the bolt head.

Under normal circumstances, never press a gear on without preheating. Some aluminum will be sheared off the gear bore and the gear will lose its press fit! The one exception is if you are running a roller cam with high spring pressures. In this application, the heating will weaken the aluminum gear and result in failure. Therefore, press

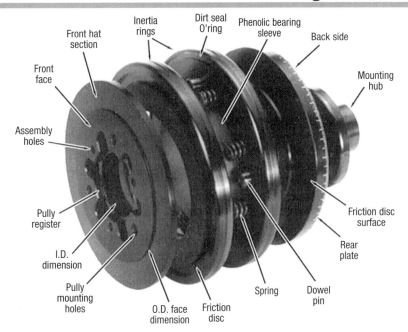

Fisher mechanical damper—exploded view.

fit the gear cold and never reuse the gear.

Note: The thrust plate with spacer ring is available from GM, part #12508079, Pioneer #PG2208 or Mellings #MG220X.

Disassembly

Crank Gear—most crank gears have twin-tapped holes so that you can use a bar-type puller. If there are no tapped holes, a jaw-type puller is needed. Always use caution not to damage the threads in the end of the crankshaft.

Camshaft Gear—place camshaft in press, support bottom, heat with appropriate torches around the hub of the gear. When well heated, apply pressure to remove gear. Using heat minimizes any loss of aluminum from bore so that the cam gear may be reused.

Harmonic Balancer (also known as a torsional damper)— this consists of two parts: the center hub with keyway and an outer balancing ring. These two components are pressed together at the factory with an elastomer (rubber) ring separating them.

Complete Fisher damper.

TCI Rattler™ mechanical damper.

View of Fluidampr Internal Components

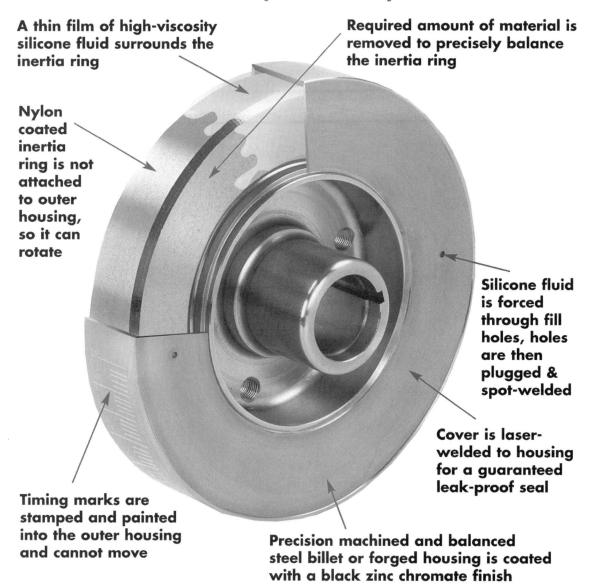

A thin film of high-viscosity silicone fluid surrounds the inertia ring

Required amount of material is removed to precisely balance the inertia ring

Nylon coated inertia ring is not attached to outer housing, so it can rotate

Silicone fluid is forced through fill holes, holes are then plugged & spot-welded

Cover is laser-welded to housing for a guaranteed leak-proof seal

Timing marks are stamped and painted into the outer housing and cannot move

Precision machined and balanced steel billet or forged housing is coated with a black zinc chromate finish

This ring is tuned for specific crankshaft frequency to minimize torsional vibration. STD-LDs use a much smaller and lighter harmonic balancer that should never be used on an HD-TD motor.

Inline sixes suffer much greater torsional vibrations than comparable V8s.

This is due not only to the inherent design characteristics, but also their long crankshaft length. The HD-TDs are affected the most, due to their long stroke.

Important Note

The HD-TDs come with two different depth keyways cut in the center hub. Some have a shallow 1/16" depth—these are useless in any performance applications, including street use. The other features a center hub with 1/8" depth keyway and this is the one to use for street performance.

Damper Selection

Street applications should use the following: GM Part

#10141202—3 sheave balancer with hot bonded outer ring.

For hot street or occasional strip, use the Self Racing Heads & Engines' mechanical crankshaft damper. This unit consists of a modified stock HD-TD damper with friction clutch action and safety plate connecting center hub with balancing ring. A modified crankshaft timing gear is also included. This is countersunk so that the damper hub moves onto the second woodruff key for a more positive retention. Although the woodruff

Exploded view of ATI elastomer damper.

key is purely for location purposes, the extra length adds surface area to enhance the press fit. This is a great unit for street/strip and still retains the stock look. It is not approved for full competition racing. It should be noted that the crankshaft snout has an O.D. of 1.255" (the same as a small-block Chevy).

Full competition engines should use one of the following:

1. **Fisher™ or TCI Rattler™.** These are mechanical crankshaft dampers. The units work through a series of clutches, springs and inertia rings to reduce torsional vibrations. This type of damper does not need to be tuned to any specific vibration frequency. The way the TCI unit dissipates vibrations mechanically creates a rattling that can be disturbing on a street-driven engine.

2. **Fluidampr®.** This unit has an enclosed inertia ring emersed in a viscous fluid. The whole thing is hermetically sealed in a housing and laser welded to ensure against leakage. Vibrations are dampened

ATI Elastomer damper.

Crank gear shown countersunk for Chevy V8 length damper (.290" deep). Straight tooth (14° angle).

when the difference in the rotational speeds of the housing and inertia ring shears the viscous fluid. This type of damper does not need to be tuned to any specific vibration frequency.

Fluidampr®.

3. **ATI.** This unit moves elastomer rings on the inner hub creating friction against the outer ring in much the same way a stock balancer functions except over a broader range.

If you choose an ATI unit, different elastomer rings may be needed for your application.

Reference points on damper are marked at 120° intervals; i.e., TDC for cylinders 1 & 6, 2 & 4, 3 & 5, as well as 45° BTDC.

The ATI unit is also available in lightweight aluminum, although some racers feel this may not provide enough damping action for an HD-TD. It may be perfect for the STD-LD engine. The 6.25" diameter balancer for the Chevy small-block V8 is used on all street and strip applications for the STD-LD series and weighs about 8 pounds. A larger 7.25" diameter balancer, which weighs about 12 pounds, may be beneficial for endurance or street applications for the STD-LD series and is a must for the HD-TD series. For all competition units, leave the hub length as received (do not shorten or modify). Note: All of the above units are approved for full racing applications.

Option

The crankshaft gear is counter-sunk to allow the damper hub to move onto the second woodruff key for more positive retention on all racing applications.

The selected balancer should be degreed and marked for important reference points; i.e., top dead center (TDC) for cylinders 1,6–2,5–3,4 and 45° before TDC #1 cylinder.

All of the competition models have at least 45° BTDC marked in one degree increments. You will have to add the other reference points. These marks have to be made in relationship to the position of the timing cover mounted timing tab. For further information see Chapter 9. When using a stock type balancer, always scribe an alignment mark between the inner hub and the outer ring to check potential movement.

Timing Gear Chart

CRANK

Early Straight Cut Tooth (14°)

1963–1965—Steel	Standard	4° Advance
GM	3836605	10028052
Mellings	2501	2537
Sealed Power	221-2501	221-2537
Cloyes Standard	2528S (Set—Crank and Cam)	Not Applicable
Cloyes High Performance	8-1018 (Set—Cast iron cam gear and 3 keyway choices of timing)	Not applicable

Later Angle Cut Tooth (20°)

1966–1989—Steel		
GM	2768986	362758 (discontinued)
Mellings	2527	2541
Sealed Power	221-2527	221-2541
Cloyes Standard	2527	2541
Cloyes High Performance	8-1016 (Aluminum cam gear and 3 keyway choices of timing) 8-1020 (Set—Cast iron cam gear and 3 keyway choices of timing	

CAM

Early Straight Cut Tooth (14°)
1963–1965—Aluminum

GM	3866727 (discontinued)
Mellings	2524
Sealed Power	221-2524
Cloyes	2524

Later Angle Cut Tooth (20°)
1966–1989—Aluminum

GM	2771369
Mellings	2526
Sealed Power	221-2526

Chapter 7

Rods, Pistons, and Bearings

- Selecting the proper rods, pistons, and wrist pins
- The correct ring selection
- Ring gap locations
- Correct rod bearings

After working with the stock block and crankshaft, the reciprocating piston and rod assemblies offer the first practical chance for the Chevy six engine builder to explore the aftermarket for trick new parts. Recall that besides a long stroke, the Chevy six features a relatively heavy piston and rod assembly. Modern aftermarket parts, especially pistons, can rapidly reduce this weight, providing an increase in longevity or usable RPM. In this chapter we'll explore the advantages and disadvantages of stock and aftermarket reciprocating parts, and how to prep those parts for duty.

Connecting Rods

The factory HD-TD connecting rods are shot peened forged steel and weigh approximately 670 grams each. The rods can be successfully upgraded and made reasonably durable, particularly if the piston weight is reduced below the factory weight of 706 grams.

Even with upgrading, these factory rods should only be used for street, mild street/strip applications or mild endurance applications in oval track racing.

Prepping Stock Rods—When factory rods are used, always:

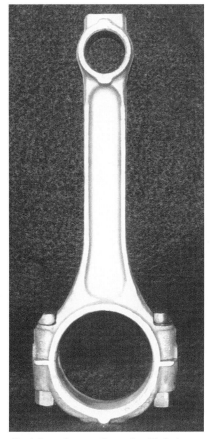

Stock forged connecting rods with factory bolts make an excellent street choice.

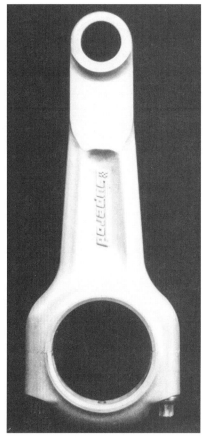

Aluminum Superod small forging HD-TD stock length, no longer in production.

1. Magnaflux each rod.
2. Replace rod bolts with heavy-duty aftermarket pieces. The HD-TD uses the same 3/8" bolt as the 350 CID small-block Chevy, while the STD-LDs use the same 11/32" bolt as the 283 CID and early

327 CID small-block Chevy. It is important to shot peen nut and bolt seats (with bolts removed). If rods are polished, be sure to shot peen afterward as polishing affects the structure of the rod adversely.

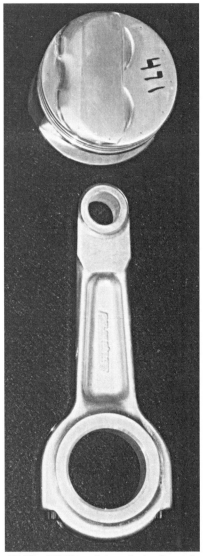

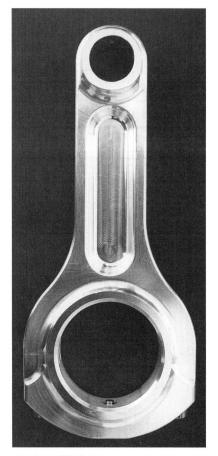

Aluminum GRP forging.

HD-TD—7.250" length large forging Superod with lightweight piston. Dome configuration for maximum compression and .800"+ lift cam. Note hand-massaged dome and gas ports.

HD-TD rods. L to R length 6.750", 7.000", 7.250", 7.350".

(Shot peen with #320 cast steel shot to an Almen arc height of .012"-.014".)

3. Rebuild rod per standard procedures.
4. Retain pressed-in pins for street or mild street/strip applications.
5. Full floating pins for drag racing, oval track and endurance racing. Never use a chrome plated piston pin—the plating process sets up micro-cracks that will lead to failure.

Aftermarket Rods—Full competition, dragstrip and short duration oval track engines need lightweight aluminum rods—small forging (550 grams) to help absorb the vibration inherent in this 4.120" stroke engine when it is twisted into the 7,000 RPM (and above) range. A beefier rod (640 grams) is also available based on a larger forging and provides extended service life. For longer duration oval track, use custom forged or billet steel rods.

Rod length should remain the stock center to center dimension—6.760" for most applications. When aluminum rods are used, ultimate engines will benefit from rod lengths from 7.000" to 7.350" center to center. The intended power range determines the rod length—the higher the RPM, the longer the rod length. The long rod moves the wrist pin higher into the piston, which stabilizes the ring package, reduces cylinder wall pressure and provides superior ring seal. This greatly reduces piston weight and hence crankshaft vibrations. The long rod also improves the rod to stroke ratio. Aluminum rods have a long history of successful use in inline engines. Billet steel and aluminum rods from a wide range of suppliers have also proven successful.

Other Considerations

1. The camshaft must be ordered on the special small .980" diameter casting or from billet. If this is not available, the standard cam core can be ground for proper rod clearance when using the small rod forgings. When using the larger rods, only a billet roller is recommended as deeper notches will need to be cut. Maintain .060" clearance between the rods and the camshaft.

2. The edge of the rod should never be modified for sufficient camshaft clearance as this significantly weakens the rod.

3. The camshaft side of the cylinder bore (looking at the block from the bottom) has to be ground for clearance when using standard or .030" overbore. At .060" or greater, there is sufficient clearance without performing this step when using Superods™ at stock length based on small forgings. Careful checking and clearancing when using the large forgings is mandatory. Use .060" clearance at all points.

4. The oil pump must be ground for added clearance with small rods (See chapter 5).

5. All of the above modifications are unnecessary when running stock length rods in an STD-LD series six, but always check carefully for any potential points of interference.

Piston Assembly

The stock HD-TD piston is a cast aluminum three ring design weighing approximately 706 grams (bare). It has a deep dish top that effectively precludes its use for any performance

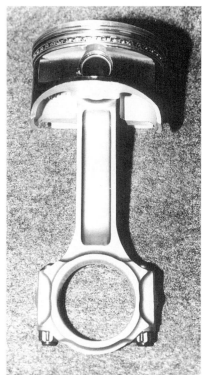

Forged steel rods for STD-LD—the choice for oval and endurance racing. 5.700" long Crower Sportsman rod with Arias flat top piston.

Billet rods for STD-LD—Crower 6.200" long with Ross flat top piston.

Camshaft—stock with rod bolt flats cast in for clearance.

Crane flat tappet cam notched for rod clearance (aluminum Superod—small forging).

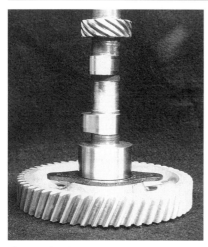

Competition Cams roller turned down to .890" to achieve rod clearance (aluminum rods—large forging).

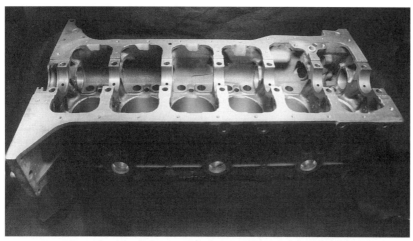

Block ground for additional rod clearance (aluminum rods large forging—stock length).

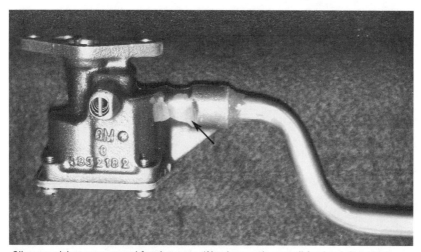

Oil pump pickup area ground for clearance. (Aluminum rods—small forgings). Note high temperature silicone to seal inlet side of pickup tube to pump body.

application due to the low compression ratio (8 to 1) produced. The exception is for street supercharged or turbocharged applications, albeit, with limited boost pressure. The piston utilizes a pressed in, heavy-duty wrist pin (143 grams). The rings consist of a 3/32" compression ring located 3/8" below the piston top, the second ring is a 5/64" and finally—oil control 3/16". Also available at a reasonable price is a cast 9 to 1 compression ratio piston originally intended for use with LP gas.

A performance piston for the HD-TD must take into account the stock piston's deficiencies, whether it is a cast or forged design.

Compression ratio

Probably the most important factor is the need for adequate compression ratio. One of the big advantages of running the HD-TD as opposed to the STD-LD series is the possibility of utilizing a flat top piston design to boost the compression ratio into the performance area (depending on the volume of the combustion chamber of the head being used)—10.5 to 1 and above. Flat top pistons are preferred, when possible, due to their lighter weight and lack of combustion chamber interference.

The weight of the piston and pin is another area for improvement. A forged piston in the 500 gram area is achievable with moderate lightening when using a stock length rod. A full floating wrist pin of H-11 tool steel brings a weight savings of about 45 grams. Together we save over 260 grams compared to stock, all while gaining a much stronger piston and pin. This not only allows the engine to accelerate more rapidly but goes a long way to reducing the stress on the crankshaft.

Ring Considerations

A further area of improvement is in ring style and placement. Going to a 1/16" x 1/16" x 3/16" ring style reduces friction and allows a wider selection of high performance ring material. Ring placement should be moved closer to the piston top compared to stock. A top ring, down about 1/8", is usually adequate for drag racing. For endurance applications, this may need to be lower—consult your piston supplier. Some racers favor a .043" top and second ring for very high RPM motors or when long rod combinations require these for proper ring placement.

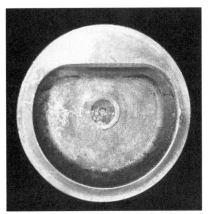

Stock HD-TD piston reverse deflector is .300" deep and gives 8.0 to 1 standard compression ratio. The .150" depth liquid propane gas (LPG) application gives a compression ratio of 9 to 1.

Note the long distance from the top of the piston to the top ring as well as the heavy-duty wrist pin of this stock piston.

Bottom view of stock piston.

When domed pistons are used, the dome must match the combustion chamber of the cylinder head. The design of the dome also must take into account proper flame travel and provide for maximum air flow at cam overlap.

Regardless of piston type, we must have sufficient piston-to-valve clearance—minimum .100" to prevent self-destruction of the valves. Minimum clearance occurs approximately 10° ATDC on the intakes and 10° BTDC on the exhausts.

Important note

Due to the long stroke and extended compression height of the HD-TD, a rather severe angle is generated as the piston reaches the bottom of its stroke. A slipper skirt piston design often localizes stress in a narrow skirt area that can lead to cylinder wall failure, even at stock bore size.

Wrist pins

Wrist pins are generally centered for pistons up to .060" oversize. Beyond this, it is advisable to offset the pin away from the camshaft side of the block to

High performance (Arias) flat top piston. Note distance from the top of the piston to the top ring, as well as the thin wall tool steel pin.

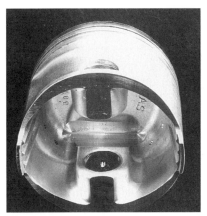

Bottom view shows additional lightening done.

Slipper skirt piston design in an HD-TD results in localized stress in the bore, which equals broken block—even at stock bore size.

Slipper skirt piston design viewed from bottom. Do not use.

Wrist pin lengths 2.850, 2.750 and 2.500.

Wrist pins various thickness: stock to ultra thin .070".

Connecting Rod Lengths and Weights

STD-LD 250 CID common rod lengths and weights (including piston weights) based on stock stroke crankshaft.

Length	5.700"	6.000"	6.100"	6.200"
Piston Weight (bare) Aluminum	520g	400g	390g	380g
	Small Forging		**Large Forging**	
Rod Weight (approx.) Aluminum	510g	520g	620g	630g
Steel forged	580g	620g	640g	660g

HD-TD 292 CID common rod lengths and weights (including piston weights) based on stock stroke crankshaft.

Length	6.760"	7.000"	7.125"	7.250"
Piston Weight (Bare) Aluminum	520g	440g	420g	400g
Small Forging				
Rod Weight (approx.)	550g	NA	NA	NA
Large Forging				
Rod Weight (approx.)	640g	670g	690g	700g
Steel billet	780g	810g	830g	840g

reduce cylinder wall stress. Offsets should only be considered for full competition use—offsets up to .0965" seem to work well.

Wrist pins for strip and super strip should be made of H-11 tool steel for maximum strength with light weight. Most performance pistons utilize .927" x 2.850" x .090" pin dimensions. Other common sizes used are 2.500" and 2.750" lengths with wall thickness ranging from .070" to .120".

Recommendations

In summary, based on a stock stroke 292 CID x .060" overbore the following combinations are suggested:

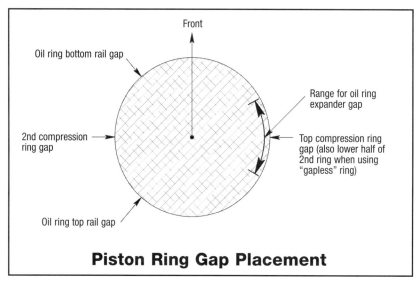

Piston Ring Gap Placement

Suggested ring gap placement for classic and zero gap ring sets.

Street

Cast flat top pistons, combined with cylinder head combustion chamber volume of 80cc would yield 10.3 to 1 compression ratio. With today's gasoline, you may want to allow an even larger chamber volume to prevent detonation. Pressed in standard wrist pins and factory forged connecting rods.

Standard replacement pistons rings 3/32" x 5/64" x 3/16".

Mild Strip

Cast or forged flat top pistons, combined with cylinder head combustion chamber volume of 74cc would yield 11.1 to 1 compression ratio.

Pressed in standard wrist pins and factory forged connecting

rods updated with aftermarket heavy-duty bolts.

Moly piston rings 1/16" x 1/16" x 3/16" for forged pistons and 3/32" x 5/64" x 3/16" for cast pistons.

Hot Strip

Forged flat top pistons, moderate lightening to 500 grams, combined with cylinder head combustion chamber volume of 64cc would yield 12.4 to 1 compression ratio. The smaller combustion chamber is achieved by using a 194 CID cylinder head.

Full floating lightweight wrist pins—H-11 tool steel .090" wall thickness/aluminum connecting rods.

Double Moly or zero gap design piston rings 1/16" x 1/16" x 3/16".

Super Strip

Forged super light flat top pistons, maximum lightening—370 grams, combined with cylinder head combustion chamber volume of 64cc would yield 12.4 to 1 compression ratio or with a very slight dome, you can achieve up to 16 to 1 compression ratio.

Full floating lightweight wrist pins—H-11 tool steel 2.500" x .070" wall thickness/aluminum connecting rods. (Special large forging length 7.250" center to center).

Dykes style top ring—1/16" cut 1/16" from piston top, no second ring, a 3/16" oil ring or double moly or zero gap design .043/.043/3mm ring package also works well.

Oval Track

Forged super light flat top pistons, moderate lightening (400 grams) combined with cylinder head combustion chamber volume of 64cc would yield 12.4 to 1 compression ratio or with a slight dome you can achieve up to 16 to 1 compression ratio.

Pressed lightweight wrist pins—H-11 tool steel 2.500" x .120" wall thickness/billet steel connecting rods (special length 7.000" center to center).

Double moly or zero gap design piston rings 1/16" x 1/16" x 3/16".

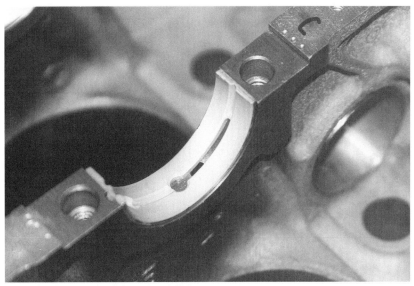

Standard replacement main bearings slotted C = Clevite.

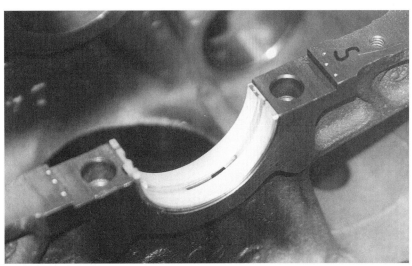

S = Sealed Power.

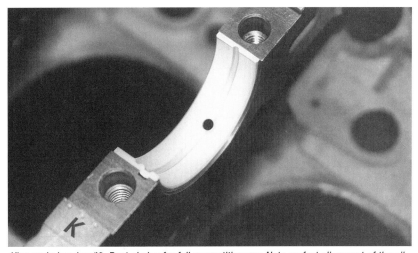

King main bearing (K). Best choice for full competition use. Note perfect alignment of the oil feed hole.

Standard replacement rod bearing—Sealed Power.

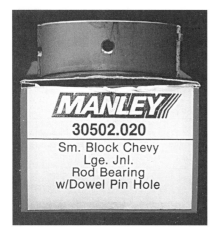

Manley with dowel pin hole for aluminum rods (same as small-block Chevy V8 large journal).

Standard GM replacement cam bearing.

Bearings

Mains—Main bearings are available from a wide range of suppliers including ACL, Clevite, Federal-Mogul, Sealed Power, TRW, King and GM. Sizes available are standard, .001",

Standard main bearing modified to align oil hole plus ditch in block to further promote oil supply.

.002", .010", .020" and .030". Some engine builders and racers feel that if you can locate N.O.S. with oil holes drilled in the exact location as in the block, these may be superior to the later replacement slotted bearing. The King bearing is the only one made now with this feature. My experience has been that both work equally well. The STD-LD and the HD-TD engines are noted for their long bearing life even under racing conditions. Do not use a fully grooved main bearing or groove the crankshaft.

Rods—Rod bearings are, likewise, widely available. The HD-TD shares the same bearing size as the (1968 and up) small-block Chevy V8 large journal engine and the STD-LD shares the same bearing size as the (1955-1967) small-block Chevy V8, giving us access to an excellent bearing selection.

Typical sizes are standard, .001, .002, .010", .020" and .030". Bearings with rod dowel pin holes predrilled for aluminum rods are also widely available.

Cam—Any name brand replacement bearings work well for both street or competition. Two different bearing sizes were used (both Clevite):
SH 399S OD = 1.990-2.0010
SH 718S OD = 2.0090-2.0110

Bearing Part Numbers		
HD-TD		
Years	Clevite	Bearing Number
1963–1970	SH718S	1 and 4
	SH399S	2 and 3
1971–1990	SH718S	All 1–4
STD-LD		
194 CID 1962–1967, 230 CID 1962–1970, 250 CID 1963–1970		
	SH718S	1 and 4
	SH399S	2 and 3
250 CID 1971–1984	SH718S	All 1-4

Chapter 8

Gaskets, Sealing, and Hardware

- Head gaskets, valve cover spacing and modification
- Aftermarket replacements for looks and clearance
- Aftermarket side and timing covers
- How to install various engine gaskets
- Tables for torque reference and recommended clearances

Nothing is more frustrating in engine building than to invest heavily in parts and machining, yet have a finished engine that leaks, or worse, requires something as major as a head gasket replacement just because corners were cut or the technique wasn't right.

Luckily, the Chevy six is supported by modern gasket technology, so we have a variety of head gaskets and other sealing solutions to choose from, and those technologies practically guarantee a tight, leak-proof engine. Furthermore, various valve and side cover options are available to clear taller-than-stock valve trains, or simply as dress-up items.

Valve Cover Gasket

Neoprene type is preferred for a high-lift cam and roller rockers. It is necessary to silicone two or more gaskets together to achieve clearance when using a stock type valve cover. High temperature silicone is not required but the gaskets should be coated and assembled and allowed to cure overnight. The unified gasket is placed over hold down studs to position it on the head. You did replace the stock bolts with longer studs, didn't you? No sealer is used on either the

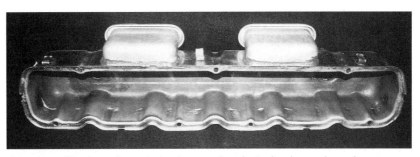

Areas to modify when using a stock valve cover in order to clear large valve springs—inside view. Stack 2 or more gaskets, siliconed together, to achieve final height clearance for roller rockers.

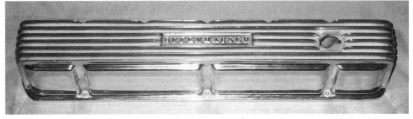

Offenhauser valve cover.

Clifford valve cover.

valve cover or the head surface—though both surfaces should be oil free.

Note: If you use a stock type replacement cast aluminum rocker cover (available from Offenhauser and Clifford;

Mercury Marine also produced covers but these are no longer in production), you will not have sufficient clearance for aluminum roller rockers without extensive modifications. Langdon's Stovebolt Engine Parts

Mercury Marine valve cover with breathers added.

Adapter and 235-261 CID valve cover on HD-TD.

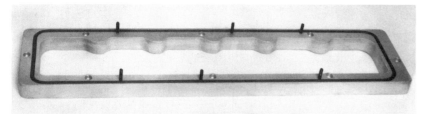

PES adapter for their cast cover.

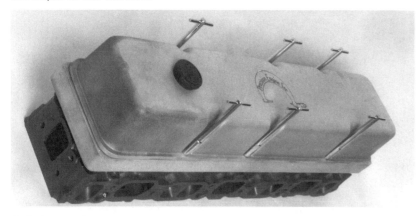

PES adapter and cover mounted.

Company has an adapter that allows the use of the older 235-261 cast covers. These covers provide sufficient clearance for roller rockers. Precision Engine Service also has an adapter which, when used in conjunction with their aluminum valve cover, clears larger valves, roller rockers and stud girdles.

Head Gasket

There are several choices when it comes to the head gasket. These choices have been street and track tested to work well with the inline six head and bolt pattern design.

1. Fel-Pro® #8006 P.T. is the workhorse. This gasket is Teflon® coated and requires no additional sealers; it is an excellent gasket. When used on a stock or mild hop-up, no re-torquing is required. When high compression (10 to 1 or higher) is used, be sure to re-torque after engine temperature has been stabilized following initial run in. This gasket has been used very successfully with an O-ringed block or head using conventional head bolts or studs. Compressed thickness is .040".

2. Fel-Pro® #1025 is the latest gasket and features pre-flattened steel O-rings around the cylinders. Make no mistake—this is a beautiful gasket for many high horsepower applications. This gasket is also Teflon® coated and requires no additional sealers. When you combine this gasket with a set of head studs, it all but eliminates the need to O-ring the block or head. It has been successfully used in supercharged and turbocharged engines in this manner. This gasket is

compatible with O-ringing for extreme engines where it may be necessary (rare). Always re-torque after the engine temperature has been stabilized following initial run in. Compressed thickness is .040"

3. Detroit Gasket #55002CS also is an excellent gasket for high horsepower applications and features a .038" compressed thickness. This gasket features a round cylinder opening, therefore some racers prefer it when O-ringing the block.

4. A reusable copper gasket is available from Clark and/or Specialty Component Engineering and is really for serious competitors only and is almost always used in conjunction with studs and O-rings in either head or block. Apply a thin band of silicone around water passageways when running water in the block or head. No additional sealers are used. Always re-torque after the engine temperature has been stabilized following initial run in. This gasket is available in a wide range of thicknesses from .032" to .093".

5. Several other gaskets have also been used successfully, including McCord #6889M and Filgar #G50005 (made in Argentina).

Head Bolts

Head bolts are threaded into the deck of the block and penetrate into the water jacket and can be a source of leaks so be sure to coat threads with Fel-Pro ProLine® Pli-A-Seal® or ARP Thread Sealer before insertion. Note: Be sure to use hardened washers under the bolts.

Sissell/Kirby custom aluminum valve cover with vents added. Note beautiful lump ports on the intakes of this head.

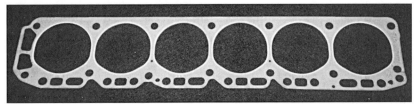

Fel-Pro® #8006 standard gasket. Note solid blue Teflon®. Note steam holes between cylinders 2 and 3, and 4 and 5.

Fel-Pro® #1025 high performance gasket. Note lack of steam holes between cylinders 2 and 3, and 4 and 5—striped blue Teflon®.

Detroit #55002CS gasket. Note round cylinder shape makes the use of O-rings easier.

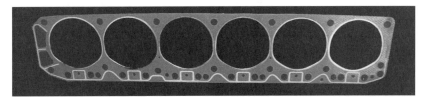

Filgar high performance gasket #G50005 (made in Argentina).

Clark copper gasket.

Block O-ring offset .065" to use the standard gasket.

O-ring cut for the head instead of the block.

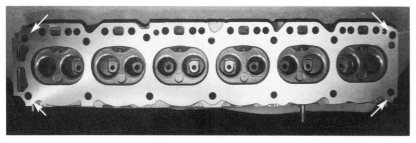

Replace end hole bolts shown with studs to strengthen these STD- LD weak points.

Exhaust Manifold

Header flange—end holes are threaded into the water jacket. Replace these bolts with studs—Loctite in place. No sealers are used on the remaining bolts.

A metal-embossed gasket holds up best for all applications—Fel-Pro® part #9786.

Side Covers

Neoprene gasket preferred, silicone the gasket to the cover so that it will remain on the cover during any subsequent removal. Grease gasket face that applies to the block surface to further facilitate easy removal. Clifford, PES, and Langdon's Stovebolt have aluminum side covers for both the HD-TD and the STD-LDs. Mercury Marine also made side covers for the STD-LDs.

Thermostat Housing

Due to the wide spacing of the retaining bolts, a cast iron housing is preferred. The gasket between the block and housing is coated with grease; this will retain the gasket during assembly. The gasket between the thermostat housing and the water neck should be coated with grease on both sides, which will allow reuse of the gasket.

Water Pump

Silicone gasket to block and grease the pump side for easy removal. For full competition engines, seal water outlet for heater connection with epoxy or tap for plug and silicone or epoxy in place. An aluminum water pump is available from Langdon's Stovebolt.

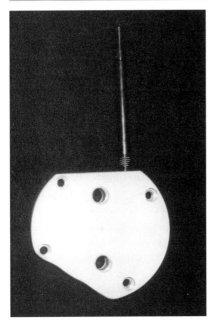

Sissell/Kirby modification for STD-LD (weakest point)—aluminum reinforcing plate, which fits through the water pump opening. Extra long stud goes through the deck and anchors into the plate. The stock head bolt hole is drilled to 9/16" to provide clearance for the stud. Stud threads entering this plate need to be about 2-1/2" long for proper torque application. Side view.

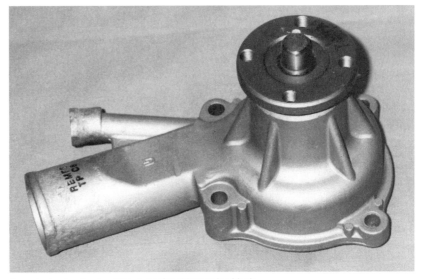

Langdon's aluminum water pump for either series block.

Langdon's thermostat housing spacer (necessary when using some of the aftermarket valve covers).

Epoxied water heater outlet (arrow).

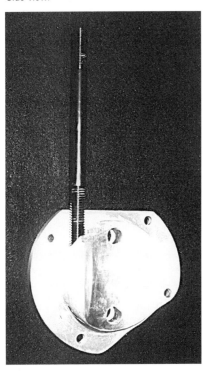

Back view of reinforcing plate.

Langdon's billet thermostat housing.

Timing Cover

Timing cover to block gasket should be siliconed to the cover and greased on the side facing the block for easy removal. The crankshaft seal presses into the timing cover without sealers and it should be replaced if there are any signs of drying or cracking of the neoprene. Always lubricate the seal with a coat of chassis grease prior to placing it over the crankshaft.

The bottom of the timing cover forms a base for the front oil pan gasket that is applied once the timing cover is attached to the block. Molded projections hold the gasket in place—no sealers are used but the timing cover surface and the pan mating surface must be oil free.

Fel-Pro® one-piece intake/exhaust gasket used for most applications.

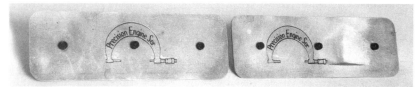

Precision Engine Service STD-LD side covers.

Langdon's HD-TD polished side covers.

Mercury Marine STD-LD side covers. This photo shows two front covers. The correct back cover can be seen at the top of page 62.

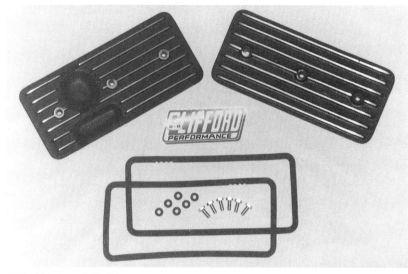

Clifford blackened HD-TD covers.

End extensions have molded horizontal projections that fit between the block and timing cover. On the pan side the ribbed extensions lie under the pan rail gaskets. Clifford has a cast aluminum two-piece cover available.

Oil Pan

Oil pan gaskets consist of timing cover portion (neoprene) mentioned above plus the side rail block gaskets of cork composite and rear main cap gasket of neoprene.

The side rail gaskets are siliconed to the block. Occasionally the gaskets will shrink after manufacture and will require stretching. To do this apply silicone to block side of gasket and, starting in the middle, center pan bolt holes and place bolts in each hole. Tighten gently to gasket surface, gradually extending to each end of the block—leave overnight to dry. Remove bolts in the morning, apply grease to exposed gasket face before final pan assembly.

Rear Main Cap

Pan gasket is neoprene. Early-style rear main bearing cap has grooves on each side and utilized a different rear main oil seal (with wings that fit these grooves). With this style cap rear pan seal requires removal of all but 1/16" of the vertical tab on

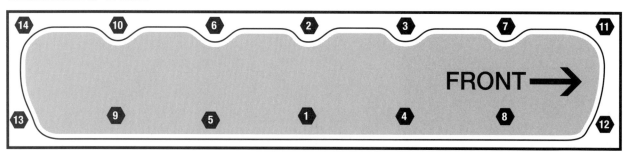

Head torque sequence—all series. Remember to torque 11 and 12 to 85 ft. lbs. for all STD-LD engines; all remaining bolts are torqued to 95 ft. lbs. All head bolts for HD-TDs are torqued to 95 ft. lbs. Ensure the water pump or reinforcing plate is attached before torquing the head.

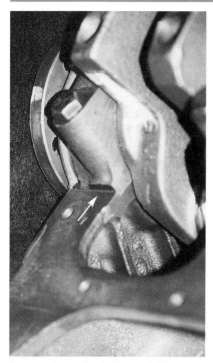

Rear cap torqued and silicone visible at parting line with block.

Plastiguage for measuring clearances of rods and mains when no other method is available. Note: when using plastiguage tighten all bolts by hand (an air wrench will give distorted reading).

each side of the pan seal.

Late-style main bearing cap has no grooves and uses a different rear main seal. Oil pan rear seal is used as is—do not remove vertical tabs. The rear pan seal is installed with no sealers with side tabs lying over pan rail gaskets.

Rear Main Bearing Seal

As mentioned above, there are two types of bearing caps and therefore two styles of rear main seals. The early-style has a groove across the flat face of the cap on each side and requires a lower crankshaft seal with wings. The late-style has no groove across the flat face of the cap and requires a different seal. Always install with the lip side with

Two-piece Clifford aluminum timing cover on STD-LD.

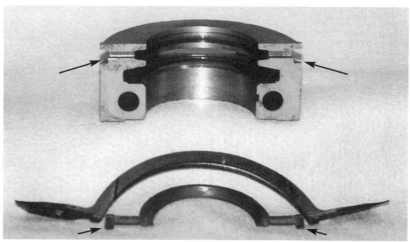

Rear main bearing cap—early-style grooved and seal with wings. Rear oil pan seal with all but 1/16" removed from vertical tab.

Rear main bearing cap—late-style with no grooves in cap. Rear seal used with full vertical tabs.

groove towards the front of the engine.

Lubricate lips with a light coating of engine oil prior to placing the crankshaft into the bearing saddles and prior to placing the rear main cap in position. Do not lubricate the mating ends of the seal. These may be offset slightly, about 1/4" to avoid the parting line of the cap when using later style seals. Before placing the rear main cap in position, place a thin layer of silicone adjacent to seal on both sides of cap or use Loctite® 515 sealer between the cap and the block (full contact surface) to prevent weeping. Do not place silicone on seal mating ends!

Important notes

1. All non-integrated manifold heads (the only type discussed in this book) use the same valve covers and various gaskets associated with the head for all series engines (STD-LDs and HD-TD).
2. The oil pans and timing covers as well as associated gaskets are the same for all series engines (STD-LD and HD-TD).
3. The side covers and gaskets are different between the two engine series. The STD-LD's are smaller. See photos for details.
4. Water pumps are different between the engine series. The STD-LD are smaller and water outlets vary depending on the application.
5. For full competition engines using 3/8" pushrods, Fel-Pro® head gaskets are the only ones featuring a 5/8" pushrod hole for proper clearance. Other head gaskets may need to be modified depending on the lift of the cam (over .700").

Bolt Torque Table

	Torque (ft.-lbs.)	Lubricant
Main Bearings	70	30 weight oil
Connecting Rod		
Stock Steel	40	30 weight oil
Forged or Billet Aluminum	70	30 weight oil
Cylinder Head (see note*)	95	Pli-A-Seal® or ARP Thread Sealer
Converter	50	Loctite® Blue
Crank/Harmonic Balancer		
1/2"	80	Loctite® Red
7/16"	60	Loctite® Red
Flywheel		
1/2" bolt	110	Loctite® Red
7/16" bolt	90	Loctite® Red
Pressure Plate	40	Loctite® Blue
Flexplate		
1/2" bolt	110	Loctite® Red
7/16" bolt	90	Loctite® Red
Rocker Arm Stud	50	Pli-A-Seal® or ARP Thread Sealer
Spark Plugs (tapered seat)	15	Dry
Intake/Exhaust Manifold	35	WD-40®
Thermostat Housing	30	Dry
Water Neck	25	Dry
Water Pump	15	Dry
Rear Block Coolant Drain	20	Anti-Seize
Starter Motor	35	Dry
Side Cover	5	Dry
Fuel Pump Block-off	20	Dry
Distributor Hold Down	20	Dry
Motor Mounts	50	Dry
Oil Pan Front & Rear	15	Dry
Side Rail	80 in-lbs.	Dry
Timing Cover End Bolts	50 in-lbs.	Dry
Rocker Cover	45 in-lbs.	Dry

*Note: With STD-LD block series—the front two head bolts should be torqued to only 85 lbs. (Be sure the water pump or the water pump block-off plate is in place prior to torquing the head. This substantially reinforces the front and deck of the block.)

Recommended Clearances

Piston to Bore	.006–.007 forged
	.0015–.0025 cast
	measured at the centerline of the wrist pin hole, perpendicular to the pin.
	Follow manufacturer's recommendations.
Piston Ring	.018" Top minimum end clearance
Piston Ring, Nitrous Oxide	.030" Top minimum end clearance
	.016" Second minimum end clearance
	.016" Third oil minimum end clearance
Wrist Pin	.0006"–.0008" in piston
	.0005"–.0007" in rod for floating pin
	(.005" end play)
Piston to Top of Block	.000"–flush with steel rods.
(deck height)	(at TDC) With high RPM/aluminum rod motor allow –.020"
Rod Side Clearance	.010" Minimum Stock Rods
	.015"–.018" Aluminum Rods
Bearings	
Rod	.0010"–.0016"
Main	.0015"–.0020"
Maximum competition	.0025" - .0030" Rod and Main
Valve Lash	typically between .010" & .038"
	Specified by cam card
Valve to Piston	
Street/Strip	.050" Minimum Intake
	.100" Minimum Exhaust
Full Competition	.065" Minimum Intake
	.125" Exhaust
Crankshaft End Play	
Street/Strip	.002"–.005"
Full Competition	.005"–.008"

Stock timing cover.

Timing cover modified to clear cam retaining bolt and washer (by PES).

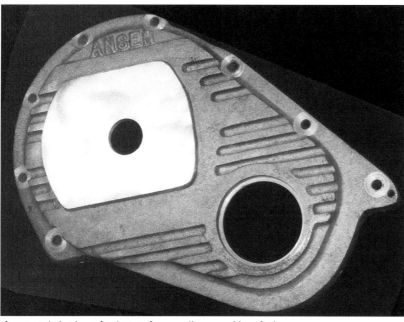

Ansen cast aluminum front cover for mounting cam driven fuel pump.

Timing cover with cam drive shown to mount Hilborn fuel injection pump. Must use small diameter (6-1/2") harmonic balancer in this application.

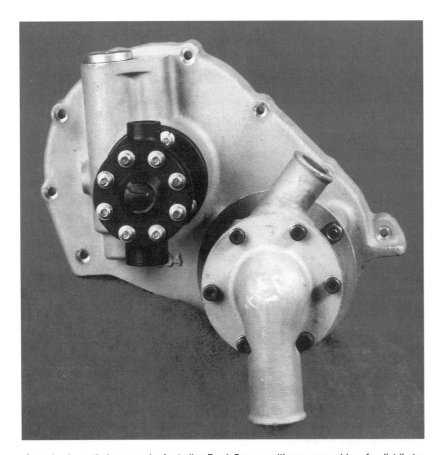

Cast aluminum timing cover by Australian Frank Duggan with accessory drives for distributor, fuel injection pump, and water pump.

Chapter 9

Camshaft Design and Recommendations

- Camshaft features and terminology
- Importance of determining top dead center
- How to read a camshaft card, and degree a cam to specs
- Setting valves regardless of cam profile
- Camshaft grinds, lifters, and pushrods

The camshaft is really the heart and soul of a great running engine. It doesn't matter how carefully you prepare your killer short block, it will be a slow motion machine without a properly designed camshaft. You need to carefully consider your goals and talk to knowledgeable people who have extensive experience with this engine series. The Chevy six has its quirky ways and trying to apply generic V8 grinds to the camshaft will produce a most unsatisfactory result. Before we provide some specific cam grinds, it is important to understand the language of camshafts and cam lobes, and also how the cam integrates with the rest of the engine assembly.

Camshaft Basics

The camshaft consists of:

1. A series of eccentric lobes that are ground to open and close the valves at very precise timings.
2. A fuel pump lobe to activate a mechanical pump to supply fuel to the carburetor.
3. A distributor gear drive, which turns the distributor shaft and hence the oil pump.

In addition, in the case of a

Camshaft terminology HD-TD Cam. Note: Eccentric lobes—intake and exhaust, fuel pump lobe, distributor gear drive and flats to clear rod bolts.

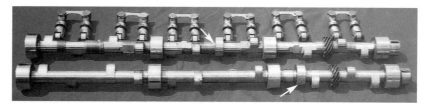

Note fuel pump lobe location differences (arrows) between HD-TD cam (top) and STD-LD cam (bottom). Cams are interchangeable, if you substitute an electric fuel pump.

Flat tappet cam notched for rod clearance. Note cam core is already cast smaller diameter than stock.

stock cast camshaft, there are flat areas between the various cam lobes to provide connecting rod clearance. The camshaft also has four cam bearing journals. The shaft itself fits in the block and is located alongside and to the passenger side of the main oil gallery when the block is viewed from the front.

Camshafts can be cast iron (flat tappet) or billet steel (roller lifter) and can be ground on

different core diameters. The stock cast cores are about 1.250" diameter between lobes whereas a steel billet roller may be as small as .850" in diameter. The smaller diameter is needed to clear HD rods. As usual, there is a trade-off in terms of camshaft flex, especially with high valve spring pressure needed for high RPM race motors. Try to stay in the .900"–.980" area and notch the shaft for proper rod clearance

71

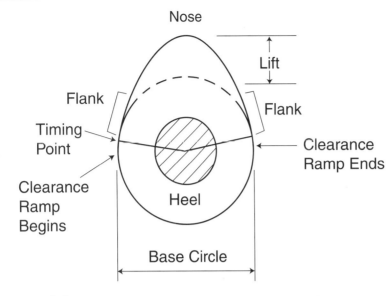

Cam lobe terminology.

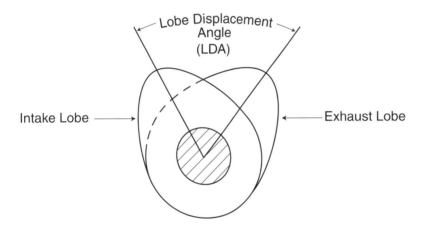

Camshaft centerline.

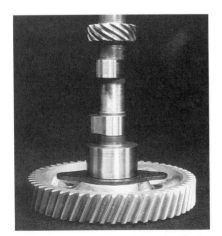

Roller billet cam with reduced diameter for rod clearance.

taken up as the lifter accelerates and begins to open the valve. Conversely as the lifter slows on the closing side it settles the valve gently back on its seat.

Flank—The side of the lobe that begins opening and closing the valve.

Nose—The part of the lobe where maximum valve lift is achieved.

Heel (base circle)—Opposite of the nose portion—lifter at rest and valve fully closed.

Timing Point—The part of the flank where the manufacturer chooses to rate the valve opening duration. .050" off the seat is the standard measurement point to compare different cam profiles.

Camshaft Terminology

Single Pattern Grind—Lift and duration are the same on the intake and exhaust lobes.

Dual Pattern Grind—Lift and/or duration are different on the intake and exhaust lobes. Generally the inlet duration is slightly (10°) shorter in duration than the exhaust.

Many of the best grinds for the Chevy six are of the dual pattern variety.

Lift—How far off the seat the valve is at maximum eccentricity of the cam lobe.

Duration—The number of degrees of crankshaft rotation the valve remains off the seat.

Centerline (lobe displacement angle)—The angular distance expressed in degrees between the intake lobe centerline and the exhaust lobe centerline.

To determine the intake centerline: take the intake closing minus the intake opening (found on the cam timing card) plus 180° divided by 2 or

IC – IO + 180° ÷ 2 = intake centerline

To determine the exhaust centerline: take the exhaust

when running roller cams and lifts over .750".

Cam Lobe Terminology

Like most specialized knowledge, being able to understand camshafts starts with decoding the vocabulary. Below are some of the basic terms associated with the cam lobe, followed by a listing of overall camshaft design terms.

Base Circle—Where the lifter rides when the valve is fully closed. This is where valves are set for proper clearance.

Clearance Ramps—Where the clearance or valve lash is

opening minus the exhaust closing plus 180° divided by 2 or

EO − EC + 180° ÷ 2 =

exhaust centerline.

To determine the lobe displacement angle, you simply add the intake centerline to the exhaust centerline and divide by 2. Most cams will be ground between 106° and 118° and 4° to 6° advanced.

If both the intake and exhaust centerline are identical, then the cam is ground straight up or in split overlap; that is, the lobes are neither advanced or retarded. If the intake centerline is smaller than the exhaust centerline, the cam is advanced and vice versa.

Degreeing—Installing the camshaft in phase with the crankshaft per the cam manufacturer's timing tag. Most race cams run best in split overlap position—neither retarded or advanced.

Positive piston stop for block without head. Note: adjust center bolt to stop piston at about .250" before top dead center.

Top Dead Center

This is a subject that is so important and necessary to understand, if you want to build successful engines, that we will review the most critical aspects here.

Positive stop when head is on the engine (screws into the spark plug hole).

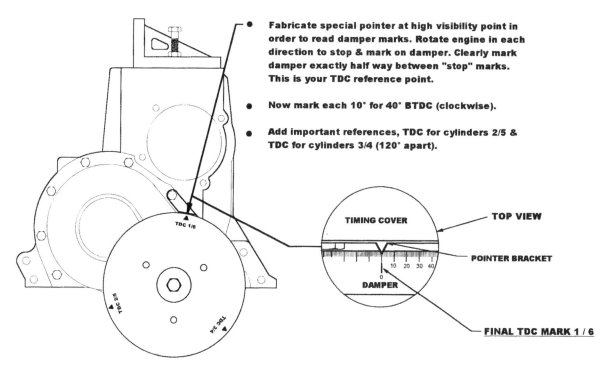

- Fabricate special pointer at high visibility point in order to read damper marks. Rotate engine in each direction to stop & mark on damper. Clearly mark damper exactly half way between "stop" marks. This is your TDC reference point.

- Now mark each 10° for 40° BTDC (clockwise).

- Add important references, TDC for cylinders 2/5 & TDC for cylinders 3/4 (120° apart).

POSITIVE STOP METHOD OF DETERMINING TDC

Positive Stop Method—Marking harmonic balancer for top dead center.

GRIND NUMBER   F-272/3874-2S-8
ENGINE IDENT.   1963 - 1984 CHEVROLET L6 CYLINDER 292 CU. IN.

VALVE SETTING: INTAKE .026			EXHAUST .026		⟶ HOT

	INTAKE @ CAM 3874		@ VALVE 678	ROCKER ARM RATIO
LIFT:	EXHAUST @ CAM 3994		@ VALVE 699	1.75

ALL LIFTS ... IE BASED ON ZERO LASH AND THEORETICAL ROCKER ARM RATIOS

CAM TIMING @ .020		OPENS		CLOSES		ADVERTISED DURATION
	INTAKE	46° BTDC		82° ABDC		
TAPPET LIFT	EXHAUST	86° BBDC		50° ATDC		

SPRING REQUIREMENTS					RECOMMENDED RPM RANGE WITH MATCHING COMPONENTS
	TRIPLE	DUAL	OUTER	INNER	
PART NUMBER 99893					MINIMUM RPM 4500
LOADS: CLOSED	120 LBS. @ 1.875		OR 1 - 7/8		MAXIMUM RPM 8000
OPEN	370 LBS. @ 1.235				VALVE FLOAT 8400

CAM TIMING @.050		OPENS		CLOSES		MAX LIFT		DURATION
	INTAKE	31° BTDC		61° ABDC		ATDC	272°	
TAPPET LIFT	EXHAUST	71° BBDC		29° ATDC		BTDC	272°	

Typical cam card.

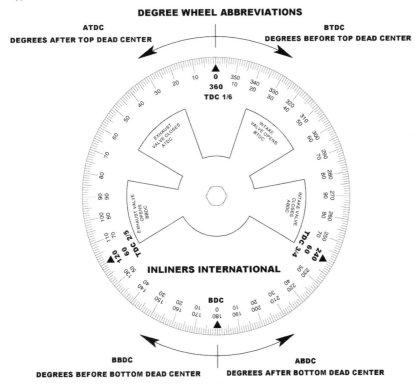

Degreeing camshaft—degree wheel abbreviations.

Camshaft gear/crank gear shown with timing marks aligned.

You must know exact top dead center (TDC). All ignition and valve timing events use this as the starting point. The most accurate way to find TDC is after the crank, pistons and rods are installed in the block, because this automatically takes into account any slight errors in keyway location, etc.

Position Stop Method

The simplest and most accurate method of determining TDC is the positive stop method. This allows you to place the pointer in the most convenient location for viewing. The harmonic balancer must be in place and the pointer positioned. Make a simple steel plate to go across the center of the cylinder. Drill and tap a hole in the center of the plate. Thread a bolt into the hole about .250" to stop the piston on its ascent. Make sure this strip is rigid so it will not bend or move when hit by the piston. Bolt the plate to the block at number one cylinder using the head bolt holes. If you are setting TDC in a fully assembled engine with the head on, use a commercially available locator that screws into the spark plug hole and acts as a piston stop.

Now rotate the crankshaft in the normal direction (clockwise when viewed from the front) until the piston strikes the center bolt. Mark the harmonic balancer at the timing pointer. Now rotate the crankshaft counterclockwise until you strike the stop again—scribe the harmonic balancer at the pointer.

Marking TDC

TDC is exactly half way between these two marks (measure the distance and divide by 2).

Measure from one mark and file a mark for TDC with a fine three corner file and stamp "0". Now measure the entire circumference of the harmonic balancer and divide by 36. This gives you the measurement for 10°. Mark each 10° interval going clockwise as you face the front of the engine from the "0" to 40°. Divide the 10° in half and mark the 5° intervals only part way across the face of the harmonic balancer. The 5° can be divided to individual degrees between 25° and 45°. Most of the competition harmonic balancers have degree marks already scribed and you'll only have to mark the 10° marks. At this time, you will also want to mark TDC for cylinders 3-4 and 2-5. These marks are to be located 1/3 of the circumference from TDC 1-6. These marks make setting the valves very easy before starting the engine. Without these important reference points, you will never be able to accurately set your timing and this will result in significant loss of horsepower.

Camshaft Card

All cams come with a specification card showing how the cam was designed to be installed. Typically, this card will list:

1. The name and address of the manufacturer.
2. The engine for which the cam was designed.
3. Grind number.
4. Part number.
5. Serial number.
6. Running (valve setting) clearance. This is understood to be at engine operating temperatures and will be specified for both intake and exhaust.
7. Net or lobe lift.
8. Gross valve lift (lobe lift x rocker arm ratio).
9. Cam timing (valve timing) at checking clearance or where the advertised duration was determined if this is specified as less than .050" lifter rise.

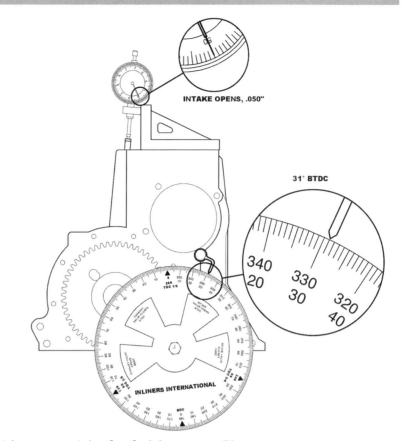

Intake opens as noted on Cam Card shown on page 74.

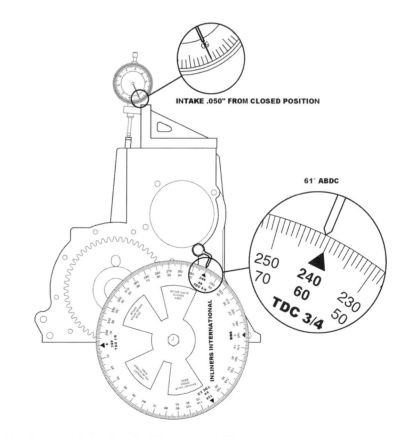

Intake closes as noted on Cam Card shown on page 74.

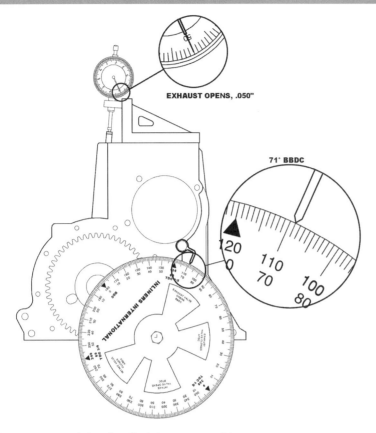

EXHAUST OPENS, .050"

71° BBDC

Exhaust opens as noted on Cam Card shown on page 74.

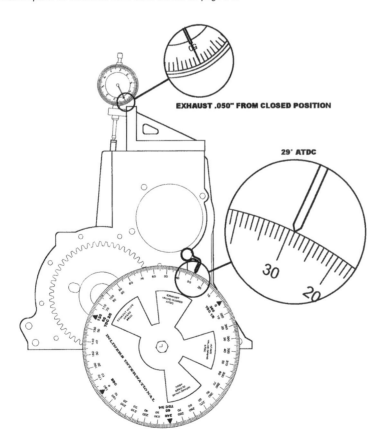

EXHAUST .050" FROM CLOSED POSITION

29° ATDC

Exhaust closes as noted on Cam Card shown on page 74.

Offset key to alter phasing in of cam, usually available 2° and 4°.

Slotted crank gear to alter phasing of cam.

Cam or valve timing is the point in the cycle that the intake and exhaust valves open and close.

10. Because of the position on the cam lobe, cam timing at .050" lifter rise provides the proper checking distance to phase the camshaft properly. If this is not on the cam card, you must contact the cam manufacturer to obtain these figures. Using less than .050" lifter rise can result in checking errors, especially for someone inexperienced. For example, at .020" lifter rise, only a .001" error can change the degree wheel reading as

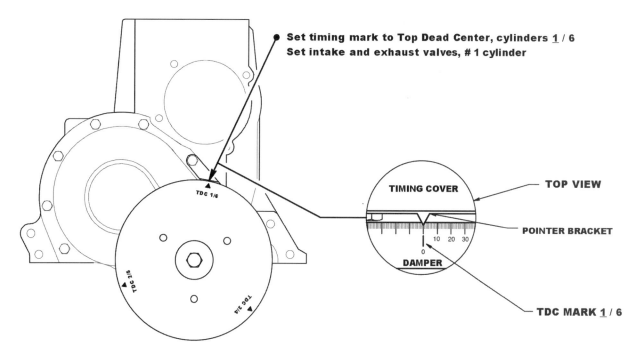

Set timing mark to Top Dead Center, cylinders 1 / 6
Set intake and exhaust valves, # 1 cylinder

INITIAL SETTING OF VALVES, CYLINDER # 1

Initial setting of valves—intake and exhaust at top dead center—firing order 1-5-3-6-2-4. Start at TDC for cylinder #1—confirm that the engine is on the compression stroke (valves closed). See photos of valve lifter positions on following page.

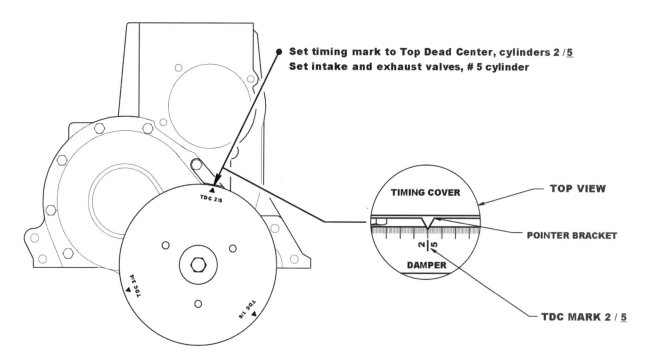

Set timing mark to Top Dead Center, cylinders 2 /5
Set intake and exhaust valves, # 5 cylinder

INITIAL SETTING OF VALVES, CYLINDER # 5

Once the #1 cylinder is set, turn the crank—mindful of the firing order. Stop at TDC for #5. Set #5 and proceed through the firing order.

Flat tappet lifters. Left to right: Stock Chevy, Ford, American Motors. The larger diameters are used when the rules specify flat tappet, but prohibit mushroom lifters.

Rocker arm stud 3/8" and 7/16" (same as small-block Chevrolet).

Note the lower position of the flat tappet valve lifters on #1 cylinder with engine at TDC of the compression stroke. Other design lifters show similar differences between cylinders #1 and #6.

Note the higher position of the valve lifters of #6 cylinder. Compare this with the position of the valve lifters of #1 cylinder. Set both intake and exhaust valves on cylinder #1.

Pushrod guide plates—Isky adjustable. These are available for 5/16" or 3/8" pushrods—the same as Chevy V8.

Head drilled from the bottom with 5/8" drill provides clearance for 3/8" pushrods. Note bevel at the top of the pushrod hole (when viewed from the top of the head) for cam lifts of .800" and higher.

much as 5 crankshaft degrees; whereas, at .050" lifter rise, a .001" error will only result in about a 1/2 crankshaft degree.

11. Duration at .050" (this will always appear less than the advertised duration).
12. Lobe separation angle (lobe displacement angle or lobe centerline). May be given for intake and exhaust separately if these are different. To determine the angle from separate readings, add together and divide by 2.

Degreeing the Camshaft

Accurately measuring cam action determines if the cam card specifications match the actual grind on the cam, in other words, was the camshaft accurately manufactured and are both keyways (camshaft and crankshaft) in perfect location? You also want to "phase" the camshaft to the crankshaft as the manufacturer designed it to be.

In order to check the camshaft, begin at top dead center. (You didn't skip that part did you?) This is the reference point for all other measurements. Next, always check measurements at the valve lifter—never at the valve. There are simply too many possibilities of error if you check at the valve.

The camshaft is installed in the block on the stock timing marks. These consist of a stamped "O" on the cam gear and a peened dot on the crank gear. Attach a degree wheel to the front of the crankshaft (the larger the diameter of the degree wheel, the easier it will be to read small increments—consider 9" as a minimum diameter to use). You will also need a 1/2" travel dial indicator to measure lifter rise.

To begin, rotate the crankshaft in its normal direction (clockwise when viewed from the front) through at least one complete revolution stopping when the number one intake lifter is on the base circle (heel) of the cam lobe, the top of the lifter will be slightly recessed in the block (see photos prior page). Be sure the lifter is lubricated with light oil and has free movement. Attach an extension to the lifter to bring the lifter movement above the head gasket surface. Position the dial indicator stem parallel to the lifter extension in both fore and aft position and side to side position. Then pre-load the stem of the indicator .050"–.080" on the lifter extension. Now rotate the crankshaft in the normal direction several times to check the runout of the base circle of the cam. This should not exceed .001" and be centered about equally on either side of the zero indicator. This is particularly important on hydraulic lifter cams!

Next, zero the indicator and look at the timing card to find the intake opening in degrees at .050" lifter rise. Rotate the crankshaft clockwise until .050" has registered on the dial indicator (this will be before top dead center)—opposite your pointer, the degree wheel should read as the card specified. Make a note of this reading and continue to rotate the crank. The lifter will continue to rise and then start down—now stop at .050" on the dial indicator before the zero reading. You are now on the

Block modifications for 3/8" pushrods. Open pushrod holes at top of block to 5/8".

closing side of the camshaft lobe. Here the reading should correspond to the cam card as X° after BDC (bottom dead center of piston travel).

The total duration between opening (before TDC) and closing (BDC) plus 180° equals your duration at .050" lifter rise. You can repeat the procedure for the exhaust lobe on number 1 cylinder. Most camshafts work best when installed at split overlap position. This means that the intake and exhaust valves are equally open at TDC. While the intake is opening, the exhaust is closing so the intake opens the same number of degrees before TDC as the exhaust closes after TDC. A cam is said to be in an advanced position when the intake valves open farther at TDC than the exhaust valves and at a greater number of degrees before TDC than the exhaust valves close after TDC. The cam is said to be in a retarded position when the exhaust valves open farther at TDC than the intake valves and close at a greater number of degrees after TDC than the intake valves open before TDC.

It should be remembered that advancing or retarding the camshaft phasing cannot alter the lobe displacement angle. The number of degrees between intake and exhaust lobes, lift,

duration and overlap are ground into the camshaft at manufacture. The thought behind changing the phasing of the camshaft is that if the cam is in the advanced position, it should enhance bottom and mid-range power and act like a cam with a shorter duration. Retarding the cam would produce the opposite effect, enhancing top end power and, in effect, acting like a cam with more duration.

Feeler Gauge Method

If the engine is already assembled, you can check camshaft phasing without a degree wheel or a dial indicator. Use a long wrench to get enough leverage—you are turning against all the valve springs and you want a smooth motion. Rotate the crankshaft clockwise as viewed from the front (normal direction of rotation) until the valves on number one cylinder are in overlap position (both valves slightly open). Stop at TDC—number six cylinder is in its compression stroke and observe that both valves are closed. Back off the rocker arm adjusting nuts until both valves are just closed (zero clearance) on number one cylinder. Lock the adjusting nuts in this position. Watching the harmonic balancer and timing mark,

Pushrod guide plates—aftermarket for Olds V8—available 5/16" or 3/8". Mounting holes must be enlarged from 3/8" to 7/16".

continue turning the crankshaft over exactly one revolution. This puts you on TDC of the compression stroke for number one cylinder. Check out what has happened to the valve clearances—they are huge! Actually, this space shows the actual amount the valves were open at TDC during the overlap period (less valve lash). Measure this gap with feeler gauges on both the intake and exhaust. If the gap is exactly the same, the cam is installed straight up or in the split overlap position. If the gap is greater on the intake side, the cam phasing is advanced and if it is greater on the exhaust side the cam is retarded.

Adjusting Cam Timing

For the STD-LD and HD-TDs offset keys are used to correct or alter the cam phasing. These are available from Moroso in 2° and 4°. Or, if you have a multi-cut crank gear, the timing can be altered by selecting the appropriate slot.

One last word of caution—changing the phasing of the camshaft—either advancing or retarding—changes the valve to piston clearance. When you advance the phasing, the intake valve to piston clearance is reduced; conversely, when you retard the phasing, the exhaust valve to piston clearance is reduced. Make sure you have left sufficient clearance (.100" minimum) to prevent contact during missed shifts, etc.

Valve Adjustment

As you will recall, the harmonic balancer was marked for key reference points, as follows: TDC and 45° before and TDC for cylinders 2/4 and 3/5. When getting the engine ready to fire, set the valves at TDC of each cylinder (the firing order is 1,5,3,6,2,4) to the cam manufacturer's specifications.

For stock or relatively mild cam shafts, this will work fine, but with long duration race cams, the lifter may be on the lobe's clearance ramp at TDC so this technique yields inaccurate results.

Therefore, after firing the engine and stabilizing the temperature, keep in mind "exhaust opening, intake closing." These magic words will ensure that you are on the base circle or heel of the cam lobe. This provides the most accurate adjustment point for setting the valves. Starting at number one cylinder, turn the engine over until the rocker arm just starts to move the exhaust valve open—now set the intake valve.

Continue to turn the crank until the rocker arm just releases the pressure on the intake valve (in other words, the intake valve is just seated)—now set the exhaust valve. Repeat for each cylinder, going by the firing order.

Recommendations

Practically every cam company has grinds for the Chevy six cylinder engine. A full discussion with a cam company representative is mandatory to achieve a proper match between your individual engine components and your intended usage. Better yet, call one of the shops devoted to these engines. They are the ones that really know what will or will not work!

In order to provide a starting point for discussion the following guidelines will prove useful for a 292 cubic inch engine; smaller cubic inch engines will need shorter durations:

Street—Advertised duration 260–270 degrees with .425–.450 inches of valve lift. Hydraulic lifter camshaft preferred.

Street/Strip—Advertised duration 270–280 degrees with .450–.500 inches of valve lift. Hydraulic or solid lifter camshaft.

Competition Only—Advertised duration 290–340 degrees with .500–.800 inches of valve lift. Solid or roller lifter camshaft.

It is important to keep in mind that the larger the displacement of the engine the milder a camshaft will act and vice versa.

Therefore a 292+ CID six can tolerate a more radical camshaft grind than can a 250+ CID engine. The flywheel will also play a role in how the engine acts. The heavier the flywheel, the smoother the engine will idle and vice versa. Another factor is to tailor the camshaft for the torque characteristics of the six cylinder—it is not an RPM machine.

Note: It is important to have a proper match of the crank and cam gear, as well as to degree the cam so that it is phased properly.

Consultants' Choices

Another good way to begin your cam selection process is to ask a Chevy inline six expert. That's what we did to compile the following list of cam recommendations. All durations are at .050" lifter rise and all lifts are measured at the valve using the stock 1.75 rocker arm ratio.

Tom Langdon

Langdon's Stovebolt Engine Parts Co.
Street—Wolverine (Hydraulic)
   250 CID part #WG1178
   292 CID part #WG1179
   Duration 194° I/204° E
   Lift .464" I/.494" E
   Lobe Centerline 110°

Pat Smith

Dyson Racing Crew Chief
250 CID Street/Strip—
   Competition Cam (Hydraulic)
   This is a custom grind, using intake lobe #260-9 and exhaust lobe #268-6-10.
Street 292 CID
   Duration 212° I/218° E
   Lift .518" I/.530" E
   Lobe Centerline 109°
Oval—Crane Cam (Flat tappet)
   250 CID Grind #F228/3067-2-8
   Duration 228° I and E
   Lift .537" I and E
   Lobe centerline 108°
   292 CID Grind #F238/3200-2-8
   Duration 238° I and E
   Lift .560" I and E
   Lobe Centerline 108°

Glen Self

Self Racing Heads & Engines
Street 292 CID—Flat tappet
   10.5 to 1 compression ratio
   Duration 244° I/258° E
   Lift .525" I and E
   Lobe Centerline 112°
Full competition drag motor
292 CID
   Duration 284° I/296° E
   Lift .890" I and E
   Lobe Centerline 111°

Mike Kirby

Sissell's Automotive
292 CID Mild Street—
   Sissell Cam (Hydraulic)
   Grind#248H
   Duration 192° I/200° E
   Lift .448" I/.460" E
   Lobe Centerline 112°
Street/Strip—
   Sissell Cam (Hydraulic)
   Grind#272H
   Duration 210° I/212° E
   Lift .490" I/.508" E
   Lobe Centerline 112°
Full competition drag motor—
   Sissell (Roller)
   Grind#E-15085
   Duration 292° I/292° E
   Lift .817" I and E
   Lobe Centerline 107°

Glen Rarick

Bow Tie Speed and Reproduction
Oval track—Ultradyne
   (Mushroom lifter)
   1/2 mile dirt track/2 bbl carb/
   250 CID
   Duration 255° I/263° E
   Lift .679" I and E
   Lobe Centerline 106°

Clyde Norwood

Precision Engine Service
Oval track—P.E.S. Custom roller
   Limited to 4 bbl carb/250 CID
   Duration 258° I/260° E
   Lift .665" I/658" E
   Lobe Centerline 106°

Leo Santucci

My favorite choices for drag racing (brackets) are:
250 CID—Full headwork and Weber carbs on both
   Moon Racing Cams FT-4B
   Duration 260° I/270° E
   Lift .576" I/.586" E
   Lobe Centerline 106°
   Moon Racing Cams FT-320/330
   Duration 262° I/272° E
   Lift .606" I/.630" E
   Lobe Centerline 108°
292 CID—Full headwork and Weber carbs on both
   Moon Racing Cams FT-6B
   Duration 272° I/280° E
   Lift .630" I/.649" E
   Lobe Centerline 108°
   Crane Cam Grind 272/3874-2S-8
   Duration 272° I and E
   Lift .678" I/.699" E
   Lobe Centerline 108°

These are solid lifter cams that work well with both automatic and four speed transmissions and with associated engine work can power an HD-TD motor in a 2800 lb. car into the 11-second bracket and an STD-LD motor in the same car into the low 12-second bracket!

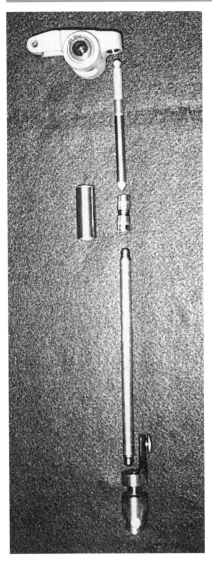

Sissell/Kirby double pushrod design for the HD-TD. Note intermediate lifter, which rides in the head.

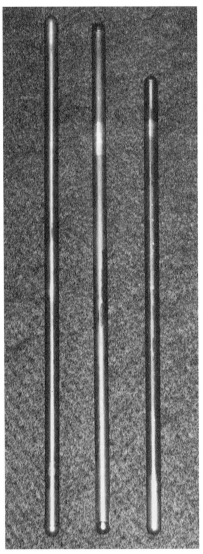

Left to right—5/16" Crane hardened pushrod for guide plates (11.565" OAL) and roller rockers, Stock push rod (11.380" OAL), Hybrid head pushrod (10.125" OAL).

Lifters and Pushrods

Valve Lifters—New lifters should always be installed with a new camshaft. Always coat the bottom of each lifter with a moly-disulfide grease prior to installation.

When running roller rocker arms in strip only engines, restrict oil to the cylinder head area with special oil restricting lifters. The preferred choice is a metered lifter from Chevy Part #5232695 (big-block Chevy V8). GM also makes a lifter (Part #523442) for the small-block Chevy V8 to reduce oil flow but

it does not work in the six cylinder. Its use will result in a flood of oil to the head and the potential for draining the oil pan, providing an instant disaster.

Hydraulic valve lifters are preferred for street use, flat tappet for bracket competition, and roller lifters for maximum performance.

There are two new lifter developments worth mentioning. One is called a cool face solid lifter—it has a .024" oil hole in the center of the lifter face. The second is a new hydraulic lifter

called a high lube, which provides 20–30 percent more oil to the lobe. Both of these features purport to give longer life to the cam and lifter combination.

Pushrods—Stock pushrods are sufficient for street use only. Beyond this, special chrome moly aftermarket pushrods are recommended. Refer to Chapter 10.

When running roller rocker arms with stock length valves, a slightly longer pushrod is required. A length of 11.570" overall (OAL) works well for the HD-TD in these applications. STD-LD use a length of 9.885" (OAL). When using .100" long valves for roller cams in HD-TD engines, use 11.550" (OAL) and for STD-LD use 9.865"(OAL). The stock diameter 5/16" is sufficient for all but the most extreme cam grinds (over .650" lift) in the STD-LD series. Beyond these lifts, it is advisable to go to special 3/8" pushrods combined with 7/16" diameter rocker arm studs. The HD-TDs should use a 3/8" pushrod for any competition application, because of the longer length of the pushrod. This combination will necessitate enlarging the stock pushrod holes in the block and head to 5/8" and the use of pushrod guide plates. Drill from the bottom of the head, using the stock pushrod holes as a guide and completely drilling out the broached slots that are in the top side of the head. The block needs additional side clearance for the larger pushrods extending down 4" from the top of the side cover rail. (Remember to order your pushrods hardened for guide plates.)

Additional clearance for the valve cover on numbers one and six cylinders is often needed. An alternative for very high lift cams is the Sissell/Kirby double pushrod design shown here and described in Chapter 10.

The Cylinder Head—
Key Element of a Super Six

- Important airflow theories
- Interviews with the experts—
    Glen Rarick *(Bow Tie Speed and Reproduction)*
    Mike Kirby *(Sissell's Automotive)*
- Photos, charts, and experimental heads

No matter what engine you are talking about, the cylinder head is the central player in producing horsepower and torque. No other engine component controls so much about the way air gets into and out of the cylinders, and because that is where the horsepower action is, the cylinder head is the key.

Let's not fool ourselves, while Chevy may have given their inline six plenty of good features, the last word in performance-oriented airflow wasn't one of them. As a truck engine, the Chevy six is oriented towards strong low- and mid-range torque, so getting it to whip up a little extra higher end horsepower takes some effort. The good news is that your effort can be amply rewarded when teamed with more aggressive camming and carburetion. Should that not be enough, there is always the hybrid head option, which we'll outline in the following chapter.

Stock Cylinder Head

The cylinder head in stock form is a cast iron non-crossflow design with both intake and exhaust ports located on the driver's side of the head.

The intake ports are Siamesed

Stock cylinder head—passenger side.

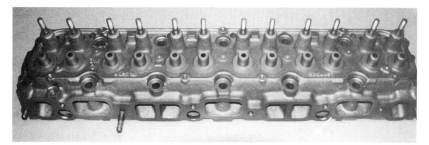
Stock cylinder head—driver side. Note pressed-in rocker arm studs.

Stock cylinder head—combustion chamber side.

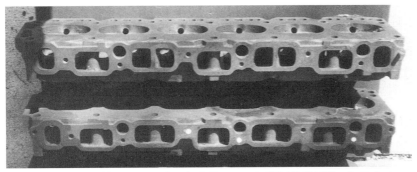

Top—regular head with separate exhausts. Bottom—early STD-LD 194 CID actually had Siamesed exhaust ports as well as well as intakes (1962–1964).

Stock cylinder head intake port with central boss—beyond street use, this boss must go!

Standard Sissell-modified cylinder head with lump port intake and modified (non-lump port) exhaust.

Kay Sissell—perhaps contemplating the first lump port design. He reportedly got the idea after viewing a big-block Chevy V8 head.

and feed through groups of two cylinders (1 & 2, 3 & 4, 5 & 6). Almost in the exact center of each of these ports is a cast-in boss, through which a cylinder head bolt passes. This location could hardly be worse from an airflow point of view!

The exhaust ports consist of separate ports for cylinders 1 & 6 and two paired groups for cylinders 2 & 3 and 4 & 5. Although these paired groups are adjacent, the passages are not Siamesed. So we do have six separate exhaust ports. The only exception is the early 194 CID head, which had Siamesed exhaust ports in the years 1962 through 1964.

The pushrod guides consist of slots machined into the head. Rocker arms are retained on individual pressed-in studs using the simple pivot ball arrangement, similar to the system pioneered on Chevrolet's V8 engines. (Rocker arms and balls are not interchangeable!)

The combustion chamber is cast for uniform and consistent shape. The spark plugs are located on the passenger side of the head. A water outlet is located on the front face of the cylinder head.

Airflow History

Early on, racers and engine builders tried to convert this head into a true twelve-port design, either by welding or

Where Are They Now?

Jim Headrick's promising engine building career was tragically ended in a highway accident at age 53 in 1996.

Kay Sissell passed away in 1992 at age 55 of a heart condition. Mike Kirby carries on the Sissell tradition to this day.

Glen Self still runs sixes and has a very successful engine building shop with his son Kevin in Durant, Oklahoma, and they still run an HD-TD in competition on occasion and are doing very innovative work on this engine series.

Glen Self and his Stormin' Six *NHRA H/MP HD-TD at Indianapolis.*

bolting in dividers into the Siamesed intake ports. Although this seemed logical, competition proved it to be the wrong direction. Before long, racers like Kay Sissell and Glen Self found more power with the Siamesed ports (with the intake port head bolt bosses removed). In fact, the head produced as much power as the twelve port Ford six head of the same era. Astute engine builders and racers noted that the Ford, with six individual intake ports, required larger Webers than the 45 DCOEs of the Chevy to produce similar power— even though the engine sizes were nearly identical. How could this be?

Meanwhile, the team of Rydell, Hope and Lang perfected the hybrid head (using two small-block Chevy V8 heads, made into an inline six head) in the late 1960s and immediately blew away the competition. NHRA subsequently banned the combination, when it became obvious that the stock type head could no longer compete.

Chevy Six Head Power Potential
Assets Versus Liabilities

Assets:

- Excellent exhaust port; good shape and good volume.

- Good potential intake port volume.

- Head accepts high performance Chevy V8 valves, springs, retainers, valve seals, screw in rocker arm studs (with modifications).

- Good structural rigidity especially on older heads made in the United States.

- Various combustion chamber sizes available (the 194 CID head being the smallest).

- Valve placement and cylinder volume allow high compression ratios with flat top piston design in the HD-TD motors.

Liabilities:

- Cast in boss for cylinder head bolt in the middle of the intake ports.

- Siamesed intake ports need extensive reworking for good airflow— i.e., "lump port" of welded, epoxyed or bolt-in design.

- Siamesed intake ports also prevent runner lengths from being "tuned" for optimum power.

- Poor head bolt layout for effective cylinder sealing.

- High rocker arm ratio stresses valve train, i.e., high spring pressures/long pushrods lead to instability at high RPM.

- Weight (the head is available only in cast iron—65 lbs.).

Airflow Comparisons

Note:

1. Measured @ 28" water pressure.

2. .600" valve lift stock head and econo-port head (street/strip).
   .700" valve lift competition ported.
   .800" valve lift competition ported. See asterisk below.

3. Modified port measurements in C.F.M.

	Intake Valve Diam.	Exhaust Valve Diam.	Intake Flow	Exhaust Flow	Intake Port Volume	Exhaust Port Volume	In/Ex Ratio %
Stock	1.72	1.50	169	122	237	86	72
Sissell Street/Strip	1.94	1.60	206	136	245	96	66
Competition Early Design pre-1985							
Non-Lump Port	1.94	1.60	217	175	262	110	81
Lump Port	1.94	1.60	249	175	225	110	70
New Design post-1985							
Lump Port	1.94	1.60	264	186	225	110	70
Lump Port (*See above)	1.94	1.60	269	188	225	110	69
Dual Lump Port Int/Ex	1.94	1.60	269	200	225	88	76

Notes:

1. Flow bench figures can vary considerably from one shop to another. Rather than taking these figures as absolute, use them as a comparison to see the changes modifications make in the ability of the port to flow.

2. Airflow is not the only criterion for a great competition head. Bigger is not always better. Note how Kay Sissell increased the velocity by making the intake port smaller with his "lump." Equally important as airflow are total port volume, runner shape and cross sectional area, mixture velocity and even combustion chamber shape can significantly alter performance.

3. The best bolt-in lump port flows in the area of 240 CFM. There is no bolt-in lump currently available for the exhaust port.

Perry and Headrick Pocket Rocket *NHRA H/MP. Where this car went, competitors feared to tread.*

Lump Port

By the early 1970s, Kay Sissell created a major breakthrough with the stock-type head by developing what is now called the lump port design. A lump of material was added to the floor of the intake ports to smooth and direct the intake charge around the short turn radius and into the cylinders. Later he added a "lump" to the exhaust ports as well.

Kay was one of the first to apply airflow technology to port design, and his work showed the importance of velocity and not just size—bigger was not better for the Chevy six head. The lump port became the standard by which every other head design was judged.

Now back to our mystery— why could the Chevy produce as much power as a comparable Ford inline despite having the apparent disadvantage of Siamesed intake ports? The answer to this question changed the way Chevy six heads were ported and the engine cammed and carbureted. It led to the next major breakthrough by engine builder Jim Headrick. When Jim and Cotton Perry decided to run NHRA H/MP, they started with a known winning combination from Glen Self (who was, at that time, the current record holder and multi NHRA event winner in his 1967 *Stormin' Six* Camaro). Glen had gotten his first cylinder head from Kay Sissell and now he did a very "six thing" to do— shared his knowledge. It wasn't long before Headrick taught his teacher a thing or two.

The Perry and Headrick drag car—the *Pocket Rocket*—a 1967 Chevy II that dominated H/MP, terrorized southern tracks and swept Competition Eliminator at the NHRA Indy Nationals in 1981.

Flow Breaktrough

Headrick's breakthrough was understanding more fully than anyone before him the real nature of airflow in the Siamesed ports of the Chevy six head. Jim was a fanatic when it came to testing and refining. Mike Kirby told me that Jim's team reputedly put over 100 additional hours into reworking the ports after he received the basic "lump port" head from Sissell.

What Jim realized was that each port did not draw 50 percent of the volume of that port, but rather, because the firing sequence never fired two adjacent cylinders, one cylinder actually was using the other Siamesed part of the port as a plenum, thus creating, in effect, a much larger port flow than one would expect. What Jim did and what was so unique for its time, was to change the timing events of the camshaft to take advantage of this "larger port." In effect, each cam lobe was ground on a different centerline so as you went from #1 cylinder to #6 cylinder some lobes were advanced, some retarded. Jim shared with me that they interbred two different cam concepts to create enhanced airflow. To my knowledge, this design was never made generally available.

There were two elements that complemented the cam design. Through extensive dyno and airflow testing, Jim could produce over 319 CFM of airflow at 28" of water on the intake side. This was unheard of in 1978!

Flow Tips

First, Jim was adamant about three points:

1. If you go smaller than a 64cc combustion chamber, you lose airflow.

"No-frills" Headrick motor put out 650+ horsepower!

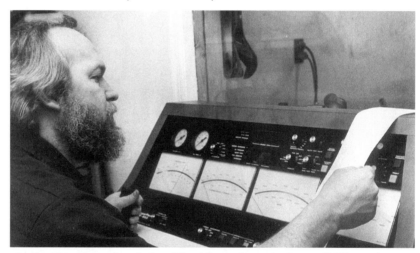

Jim Headrick—the genius who found the airflow and camming to run a 3,350 pound Chevy II (HD-TD powered) car into the low 10-second range on gasoline.

Perry and Headrick's work culminates in their complete domination of Competition Eliminator at the NHRA US Nationals in 1981. Cotton Perry is all smiles holding the team's trophy.

Race Engine Design full competition head—lumps on both intake and exhaust.

Race Engine Design experimental head. Note how much the exhaust ports are raised. Note: This design was not successful.

Sissell's pattern machine—starting to rough-out another lump port head.

Close-up of intake port being cut. Note above the port filled to provide room for the sealing plug.

Bolt-in lumps (Precision Engineering Service) for the intake port. Top view. No bolt-in lumps were ever made for the exhaust port.

P.E.S. lump plate. Bottom view. These plates attach with countersunk screws from the head deck.

2. Maximum size valves are:
   Intake 1.970"
   Exhaust 1.625"
   The bore size imposes these limits.
3. Velocity in the ports is critical.

Secondly, in order to support this airflow, more carburetion was needed as the power band moved into the higher RPM ranges (8,000–10,000 RPM). Several custom made 3 x 2 sheet metal manifolds were devised and, after extensive airflow testing, Jim settled on one that proved to provide more power than any other system available at the time.

Remember, these engines were all-out drag racing motors running in very tight power bands for limited times. Still, it is important to understand these fundamentals of power production—even though few of us would strive for this high level of horsepower production (estimated at over 650 HP).

Keys to Modification

There are only a few shops that have demonstrated, over the years, their ability to provide outstanding airflow utilizing the stock Chevy six head. I cannot recommend too strongly the wisdom of drawing on their expertise in preparing your head for its intended use. The time it will save is well worth the expense—for, without proper airflow, nothing else will work—Period! The power any engine makes is primarily a function of the amount of air it consumes! In my opinion the best shops to deal with these issues are:

1. Sissell's Automotive
2. Self Racing Heads & Engines
3. Race Engine Design
4. Bow Tie Speed and Reproduction

Before any modifications are done, make sure you have your head pressure tested. It is wise to have this repeated after all modifications, especially if welding has been done to create a lump port design.

Regardless of your intended usage, getting good valve work is essential. If your shop isn't using a dial indicator to check the seat run out and if they're not checking the valve heights, you may want to look elsewhere. According to Mike Kirby, if this area isn't done properly, you can lose 15-30 CFM of airflow on a competition head.

Levels of Modification

Street

It is very important to maintain airflow velocity and therefore, those contemplating doing their own modifications should concentrate on excellent valve work. This alone can gain 15–20 CFM. Blending and bowl work,

Cutaway view through the intake valve showing port shape—stock head. Note head bolt boss in port.

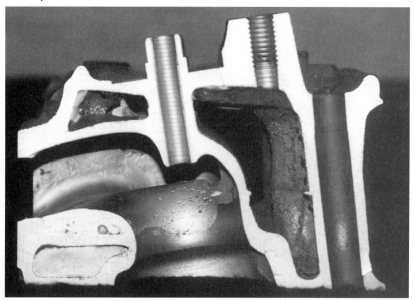

Cutaway view through the intake valve showing modified port shape—lump port head.

especially the venturi radius leading to the valve are of critical importance. Do not just cut straight in. According to Mike Kirby, this is probably the most common mistake he sees on home-ported heads. Look at what the factory did and don't try to out-guess them.

It is critically important to blend the bowls and short turn radii down to the valve guides. What we are seeking to achieve here is to create a lot of airflow at low to medium valve lifts. We want to maintain a .275" difference between the intake valve size and the bottom of the valve bowl throat. For example, if we replaced the stock-sized valves on the intakes with 1.94" diameter valves, we want the

Frontal view of lump port intake with access port to new tapered head bolt.

Cut-away view through the exhaust valve showing port shape—stock head.

head based on stock-size valves which is reasonably priced for this application. Replacing the stock-size valves is worth the additional expense if the budget permits.

The head bolt boss in the middle of the intake ports should be shaped like a wing, but left in place. Removing this boss will gain about 5 CFM on a stock valve size head, but the subsequent loss of velocity in the port will more than offset the gain.

Hot Street and Strip

Here you will want to remove the bosses from the intake ports and countersink the holes for short Allen bolts. Drill and tap an access hole above for a 3/8" pipe plug. Definitely do use 1.94" intake and 1.60" exhaust valves. Perform the same careful valve work and blending as before. Match the port openings to a Fel-Pro® #9786 intake/exhaust gasket.

Remove pressed in rocker arm studs and machine pads lower to achieve the correct height when using big block 7/16" screw-in studs.

For hot street/strip, shoot for a combination of flat-top piston and chamber volume of about 84cc's so as not to exceed 10 to 1 compression ratio.

Sissell's offers a competition series porting with boss removal which works well in these applications.

Of course, if money is no object, go for a complete lump port head. The lump port design pioneered by Sissell back in the 1970s and refined on a continuous basis, consists of a lump of material added to the intake ports to redirect the airflow and increase the velocity in the ports. This design is so efficient, it works well even on a hot street car—if you can afford the cost.

throat .275" smaller or 1.665". This differential creates a venturi effect promoting high velocity at the valves and tremendous airflow in the .200"–.500" valve lift area.

Intake valve angles for the head:

- 30° or 38° top cut .040" wide
- 43° or 45° second cut

- 60° or 52° bottom cut blended
- Exhaust valve angles for the head:
- 37° top cut
- 45° second cut
- 57° bottom cut

Rocker arm studs and stands can be left as is for street use.

Sissell's offers an Econoflow

When using a lump port on a street engine, bear in mind that the new short cap screws in the intake ports are more subject to thermal cycling, and should be Loctited in place and checked regularly. An alternative to the welded lump port is a bolt-in lump developed by Precision Engine Service. One can also be fashioned out of high-strength epoxy, although it is questionable how well this would hold up for long term street use.

Full Competition Oval Track and Strip

Full competition oval track, where durability is a prerequisite and RPM is typically lower, requires a somewhat less radical approach to maximum performance head work. The head casting itself is limiting in the bowl area—grind too thin in this area and your head will have a short service life. In general, the exhaust port is not as critical in oval track engines due to their relatively lower RPM (as compared to drag race engines). Of course, a lump port is needed on the intake after boss removal.

Bow Tie's Prep—Glen Rarick, a noted oval track engine builder (Bow Tie Speed and Reproduction), describes the head operations he performs:

"We select a 230–250 cubic inch head core made in the U.S., have it cleaned, magnafluxed and pressure checked. If it passes these tests, we then mill out for .500" O.D. bronze valve guides and we offset both the intake and exhaust spacing .030" towards the center of the combustion chamber (this helps reduce the shrouding effects of the chamber and cylinder wall). Of course, we mill out the three center intake bosses and drill and tap the top access hole to 3/8" pipe thread—sometimes we use 1/2" because this allows easier access to the short head bolt and it makes it

Cutaway view through the exhaust valve showing port shape—lump port head.

Cutaway—combustion chamber side. Note treatment of valve guide area, as well as braze added to the chamber wall on both sides of the spark plug (to reduce chamber cc's).

Shaping of cylinder head boss into a wing shape for street and mild competition use.

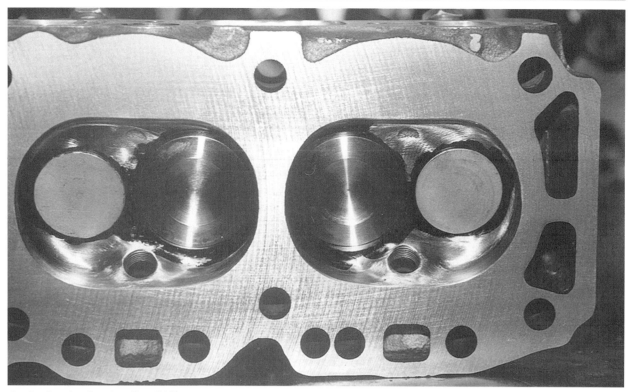

Combustion chamber view. Street/strip.

Hot street and strip—head bolt bosses removed and gasket matched to Fel-Pro® #9786.

Closeup of non-lump intake port.

Spring Pressures vs. Cam Duration

Hydraulic Lifter

Duration	Seat Pressure	Open Pressure
195°	90 lbs	230 lbs
195°-220°	100	250
225°-240°	120	300
245°-255°	125	325

Flat Tappet Lifter

223°-235°	110 lbs	280 lbs
240°-250°	120	300
255°-290°	125	350

Roller Lifter

260°-275°	180 lbs	550 lbs
280°-295°	200-260	700-800

Note: Camshaft durations are at .050" of lift. Pressures are in pounds.

easier to machine the floor of the port parallel to the deck. If we do use a 1/2" hole, we have to flow in extra material in this area.

"We remove the valve guide humps completely in the exhaust ports and about 90 percent in the intake port. After we install our bronze valve guides, we taper on

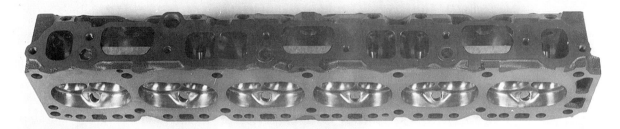

Bolt-in lump ports installed in head. Note shape of port requires special gasket (from P.E.S.) and manifold modification to match or use P.E.S. 4-barrel intake manifold.

Epoxied-in aluminum lump ports of Gregg Kramer's head.

the port side from .500" to a steeple shape. We hone the guides for a .002" valve stem clearance. Teflon® oil seals are fit for both intake and exhaust valves. Blending of the bowls and short turn radii are very important—plenty of extra time is spent here. We then perform a triple angle valve job leaving a .060" wide seat for the intake (with a 1.94" valve) and a .080" radius exhaust seat (with a 1.60" valve). We also grind and radius the combustion chambers to match a Fel-Pro® #8006PT head gasket and polish the chamber with a 240 grit abrasive roll.

"We drill 3/16" holes to provide extra cooling of the deck and head—these match similar holes previously drilled in the block deck surface. The pushrod guide slots are drilled out from the deck surface side (the stock size hole is drilled all the way through, eliminating the slots on the opposite end.

"On the top of the head, we grind and contour and groove oil return passages. Sometimes we

Gasket matching by Ron at Sissell's.

Spring Availability

Sissell Pro Series	Dia.	Spring Tension @ Installed Height				.030" off Coil Bind
		2.00"	1.94"	1.875"	1.812"	
470	1.437"			160lbs		415lbs
480	1.437"			145lbs		450lbs
670	1.550"	135lbs	150lbs	165lbs	200lbs	450lbs
850	1.550"	180lbs	200lbs	225lbs	250lbs	580lbs

Manley	Dia.	Spring Tension @ 1.900" Installed Height	Maximum Valve Lift
22448	1.625"	240lbs	750 lbs (at 1.150")
22438	1.625"	285lbs	800 lbs (at 1.200")

Close-up of intake and exhaust ports. Note how well blended-in the lump is.

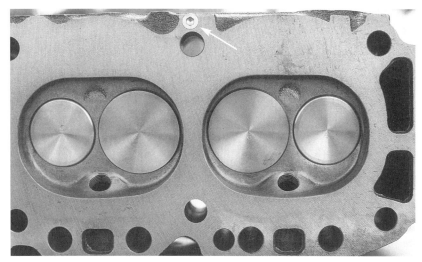

Combustion chamber. Note 2.02" intake and 1.60" exhaust. Also note countersunk Allen screw in the head to positively retain the lump.

taper the return holes as well. Next, we remove the pressed in rocker studs and machine down the mounting pad to achieve the proper height to install big-block Chevy V8 screw-in 7/16" studs. The amount removed (.100"-.400" depends on the length of the valves used. Be sure to chamfer the hole after it is drilled to proper size for the new 7/16"

NC thread—a 45° tool is used leaving a bevel of about 1/8". If you neglect this operation, you will be in danger of cracking the mounting pads. We use P.E.S. guide plates for 3/8" pushrods. The valve spring pads are enlarged for bigger diameter springs as well. We also make our own stud girdles to stabilize the valve train. These are made of

1/2" x 1-1/2" rectangular aluminum bar stock using V8 stud girdle locks and nuts with the two end nuts utilizing a snap ring to maintain the proper height of the bar off the rockers.

"Next, we install our own cast "lump" (or ones from P.E.S.) into the intake ports. Ours are made with a radius to epoxy in. P.E.S.'s bolt in from the deck surface. We have never experienced failures with the epoxy method. We fit the Allen head bolt in flush with a flat washer and install this so the head of the bolt is flush with the top of the "lump" plate. On the top of the head, our access hole to the Allen bolt is fit with plugs to seal and are marked and contoured for each port so that the bottom of the plug is a perfect fit and this forms a flat roof for each port.

"Most heads (not the new Mexican replacement) can be flat planed up to .100", but we always try to take as little as possible to retain maximum deck strength.

"We also always take care to align the cylinder head combustion chamber with the bore of the block. You can visualize this by mounting the head to a bare block and looking at it from the bottom of the block. If needed, we would use offset pins to align the head properly (typically .030" to .090").

"We build mostly STD-LD single, two and four barrel motors due to restrictive racing

Epoxied lump port (not recommended for street use). This head was designed for turbo drag car on methanol.

rules in our area, but certainly this idea would work on an HD-TD—that is angle milling of the head. We have prepared many 250 CID engines .030" over (254 CID) for use with flat top pistons and easily achieved 12 to 1 compression ratio by angle milling the head (194 CID) .125" with the heavy cut in the spark plug side of the head. Of course, the head bolt holes are reamed straight so as to be perpendicular to the block deck. The head bolt pads are also machined perpendicular."

Sissell's Prep—Mike Kirby (Sissell's Automotive) describes the preparation of a full-out drag racing head with double lump ports (intake and exhaust). "Our first operation is to remove the posts in the intake ports, pressed in rocker studs and all freeze plugs. We start with a new GM replacement head, which comes with an 84 cc combustion chamber and hardened valve seats. These are now manufactured in Mexico—the decks are thinner than the older ones that were made in the US. We start with these because it is much better to furnace braze in the lump ports on a brand new casting.

"Before we braze, we take several measurements as baselines—typically, one on each end and one in the middle in order to judge the degree of warp

Top of the head shows 3/8" screw-in rocker studs and stock broached push rod guide holes—all that is necessary on a low RPM turbo motor.

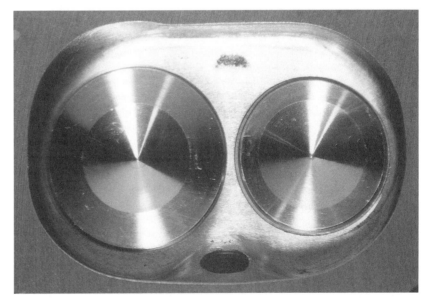

Combustion chamber with 1.94" intake and 1.60" exhaust valves. Note relief of the chamber wall is necessary to maximize intake flow.

Bow Tie Speed and Reproduction full competition oval track head with epoxied-in lump ports for STD-LD.

Bow Tie Speed and Reproduction experimental head—angle milled .070" off passenger side—intake ports raised 5/8"—exhaust ports spread 3/8" and contoured to shape of the end exhaust ports.

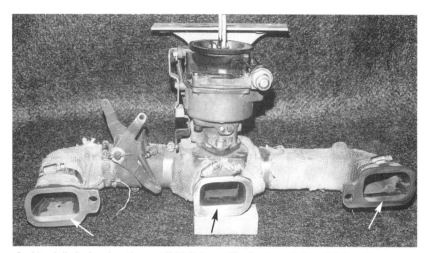

Oval track limited carburetion manifold. Note modification to ports to match lump intake in head.

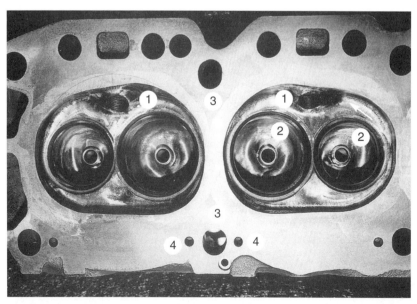

Bow Tie Speed and Reproduction finished combustion chamber. Note shape of combustion chamber (1). Valve guides (2). Elongated head bolt holes (3) in order to accommodate .090" offset dowels (to align combustion chamber with cylinder bore). Additional cooling holes (4) next to head bolts on driver side of head.

from the brazing process. With these measurements, we can minimize our final cut. Typically the heads warp from .005" to .020" After brazing and stress relieving, we level the deck and also cut the intake/exhaust face flat.

"A special tracer three axis cutting machine then hogs out the head to approximately 80 percent from both the intake and exhaust manifold side as well as the combustion chamber side. The combustion chambers are also machined for uniformity and to unshroud the oversized valves. The head pattern is one we have spent countless hours on and is known to exhibit excellent airflow characteristics. Bronze valve guide liners are installed and we narrow the sides— shortening the length of the guides does not improve flow.

"At this time, we machine in the lumps for tapered 1/2" Allen bolts and corresponding 3/8" pipe plugs in the roof of the port for access holes to these bolts.

"We machine the spring pads for 1.625" diameter springs (for roller cams) and cut the rocker arm mounting pad .300"-.400" for use with .100" long valves. We drill and tap for 7/16" big-block Chevy V8 screw-in studs. We use our own guide plate for either 3/8" or 5/16" pushrods depending on the application, i.e., single or dual pushrods.

"We drill out the cast in pushrod guides. Intake valve size is 1.96". Valve angles in the head are 30°, 43°, 60°—on the valve 30° and 45°. The exhaust valve size is 1.60". Valve angles in the head are cut to 37°, 45° and 57°. The valve angles are cut 20°, 35° and 45°. No modifications are done to the oil drain back holes.

"The balance of the porting is now done by hand—especially critical is the short side radius down to the guide. On the intake side, the air likes to come straight off the seat with the brazed lump design but if we grind too much here, it weakens the head so we don't come straight off the 45° angle of the seat, but leave a little of the 60° angle. The casting limits us here. The exhaust port is blended considerably, even on the short turn radius, so we end up with about .030"–.040" of the bottom bowl cut. Of course, throughout the process, we are constantly striving to equalize each port on the flow bench. All valve work is completed and dial indicated for run out. Spring heights are established.

"The manifold side of the head ends up a match to the FelPro® intake/exhaust manifold gasket.

"When everything is finished, we polish the intake ports with 40 grit, the exhaust and combustion chamber is flutter polished with 80 grit and, finally the head is painted.

"This complete head, ready to bolt on (less rocker arms) is known as our Pro Series with "lump" exhaust option."

Valves, Springs and Associated Parts

Springs—Z-28 Chevy V8 springs with stock retainers, keepers, and stock length valves can be used on hot street cams with up to .480" lift, either flat tappet or

Experimental head. Performance results are unknown. Note radical intake port location and size as well as extreme exhaust port work.

Intake port detail with modifications to mount manifolds shown below.

Custom three 2-barrel intake manifolds for huge 50 DCO Webers for this head.

hydraulic lifters. For flat tappet cam lifts up to .640", special springs are available. Consult with one of the aforementioned shops or one of the cam companies.

The chart on page 92 relates seat and open valve spring pressures required for various camshaft designs and applications.

Note: Camshaft durations are at .050" of lift. Pressures are in pounds.

Valves—.100" longer valves are used primarily with roller cams. They need much more spring pressure and larger diameter (1.550" to 1.625")

springs as well as higher installed heights. Needless to say, use only premium quality valves. (This is not the place to economize.)

Retainers—Standard retainers for other than hot street are chrome moly. For full-out competition titanium retainers are a good option if they can fit your budget.

Keepers—Keepers for retainers are machined and hardened for lifts at .540" or hotter. For roller cams, a 10 degree retainer and keeper is recommended.

Valve Caps—Valve caps ("Lash caps") are used on

Full competition head. Note enlarged spring pockets. Rocker stands modified for 7/16" screw-in studs, .100" long valves and high lift cam (.800") and 3/8" pushrods. Note top of valve guide cut for valve seals.

Early Sissell non-lump port head. Note pinned rocker studs.

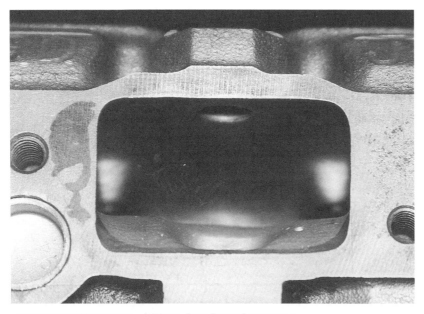

Closeup view of intake port—full lump. Race Engine Design head.

titanium valves to protect the ends and to give a little more area for the roller rockers to ride.

Valve Cover—Precision Engine Service makes an adapter and aluminum valve cover to clear stud girdles, .100" long valves and 1.625" diameter springs. Mike Kirby made a neat adapter to the head on one side and big-block Chevy V8 valve covers shortened and spliced on the other for those who want to make it themselves. Mike also has a competition custom valve cover, if you really want to splurge.

Langdon's Stovebolt Engine Parts Co. also makes an adapter which allows the use of the early Chevy six "235-261" cast aluminum or stamped steel cover, which will also clear all the goodies.

Pushrods—The best choice for most applications is a 5/16" .075 inch wall thickness chrome moly design. For full competition high RPM applications, a 3/8" design is preferable—a tapered design may further enhance stability. (See chapter 9 for pushrod lengths.) Another choice for full competition is a two-piece, designed by Kay Sissell and currently available from Mike Kirby. The unit consists of a 7.015 inches long 3/8" push rod from the lifter up to a smaller intermediate lifter located in the head. From there a 3.640 inches long 5/16" push rod activates the rocker arm. This two-piece design has proven to provide excellent stability and durability in several years of testing in high RPM HD-TDs. The big disadvantage of the two-piece is the much greater cost.

Rocker Arms

The stock rocker arms are individually stud mounted and each unit consists of a stamped steel rocker arm, a pivot ball and

Intake port looking at one valve. Race Engine Design head.

an adjusting nut. Each rocker arm is held in proper alignment by a slot in the head, which limits pushrod movement. The nominal ratio is 1.75 to 1 on both the intake and the exhaust rocker. The stock stud diameter is 3/8".

The stock rocker arm arrangement is simple, light-weight and proven reliable over millions of street miles. When you decide it's time to do headwork to increase the airflow, it is time to change to screw-in studs, guide-plates, and enlarge the head opening for larger pushrods. All of these operations are easily done while other head work is being performed. So, by planning ahead, you can continue to run stock rockers or go to Comp Cams' High Energy (roller tip – ball pivot) rockers with the intent of later upgrading to a full roller rocker and larger stud. The threads cut in the head during this operation are the same for either size stud. The screw-in studs are the same as those used for the small-block and big-block Chevrolet V8. When going to roller rockers, I recommend using the larger 7/16" diameter big-block studs. These will provide less flex and are adequate for 99 percent of all applications. Ultimate engines may benefit from shaft mounted rockers when running valve lifts over .850".

Rocker ratios between

Closeup view of exhaust port. Race Engine Design head.

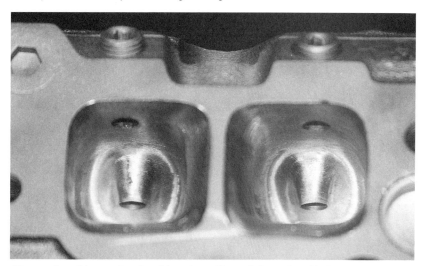

Closeup view of lump exhaust port for valve guides and shape. Race Engine Design head.

Closeup view of lump exhaust port for HD-TD. Race Engine Design head.

1.70 to 1 and 1.90 to 1 have been tried with no significant advantage found over 1.75 to 1. Big-block Chevrolet rockers of 1.70 to 1 can be used as well as rockers made specifically for the Chevy six.

Important points:

1. Regardless of the type of roller rocker you choose, always verify the geometry of the rocker. This geometry (the way the roller sweeps

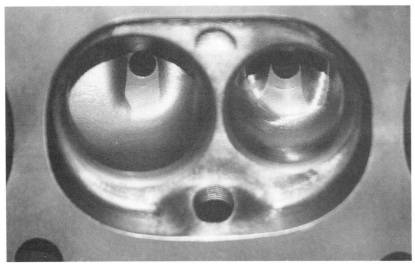

Combustion chamber, intake and exhaust seats. Note shape of the valve guides and smooth transition from valve seats to ports. Race Engine Design head.

across the valve stem) varies significantly from one manufacturer to the other. Always confirm that the roller starts on the inside edge of the valve stem (towards the stud) and rolls across the stem so that at 50 percent of the lift of the cam, the roller is exactly in the center of the valve stem.

2. Confirm the following clearances:
   a. Between the stud and the slot in the rocker. This can be done on a fully assembled engine by turning over the engine by hand and placing a

Experimental Sissell/Kirby raised runner head-intake and exhaust. Note extensive use of braze.

Port view of road racing head from Argentina for a destroked 194 CID engine.

Shaft rocker arm assembly for the Argentina head.

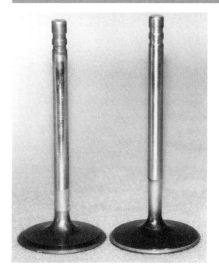

Stock length valve vs .100" long valve— longer valves are used for roller cams with large springs, which require greater installed height.

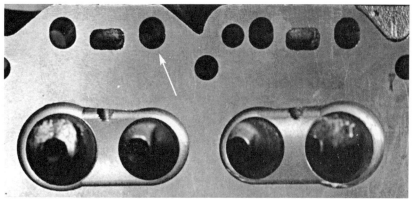

Combustion chamber of the Argentina head. Note the small chamber size and elongated and enlarged pushrod holes.

Standard retainer vs. chrome moly and titanium.

Valve spring comparison. L to R: 1050—triple wound spring. Max all out 1.625" diameter wound for extreme lifts in the .760"-.850" range. 950—double wound roller spring with spacer. 1.550" diameter. 850—double wound roller spring with spacer. 1.550" diameter. Both of these are for valve lifts up to .750" of lift. 480—flat tappet and hydraulic spring. 1.437" diameter. 470—flat tappet and hydraulic spring. 1.437" diameter. Z28—flat tappet spring. 1.250" diameter for valve lifts up to .600". Stock spring. 1.250" diameter for valve lifts up to .500".

Keepers—standard vs. 10°.

STD-LD with Jesel shaft rocker arms 1.80 ratio intakes and 1.75 ratio exhausts on Glen Self engine.

bent paper clip in the slot of the rocker. If the paper clip is not pinched after a complete rotation of the engine, you will have enough clearance (.060–.080") If it does pinch, lengthen the slot of the rocker or purchase long slot rockers.

b. Between the bottom of the retainer and the top of the valve stem seal.

c. Between the edge of the retainer and the inside body surface of the rocker arm.

d. Pushrod clearance on the head and block as well as the pushrod guide plates. If you are running a high horse-power/high RPM motor, allow extra clearance for the flex encountered at high RPM.

3. Always check the spring for coil bind at full camshaft lift.

In conclusion, any motor with a high lift cam (.550" or more) needs, at a minimum, long slot rockers. Cams above .600" lift require roller rockers so always plan to make this conversion while other head work is being done.

Roller rockers and long slot steel rockers are available from a number of sources including Clifford, P.E.S., Sissell, etc., as well as from various cam manufacturers.

Shaft mounted roller rockers, 3/8" pushrods and oil spray bar. All by Walt Skoczylas.

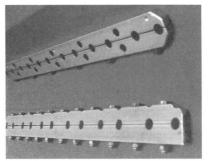

Rocker arm stud girdles, top girdle bears the mark TRC, bottom girdle by Ridgeway and bears the patent #3870024.

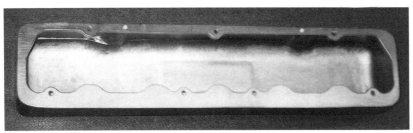

Valve cover from Sissel with adapter—this will clear large spring roller rockers and stud girdles.

Stovebolt adapter to use early "235-261" Chevy valve cover. There is plenty of clearance for valve gear and it retains a nostalgic look.

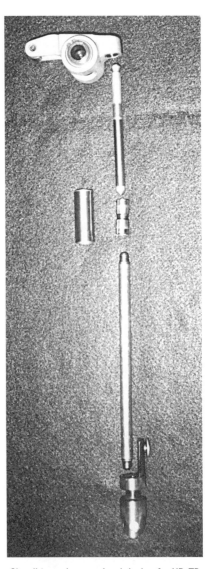

Sissell two-piece pushrod design for HD-TD. Note intermediate lifter which fits in the head. Probably overkill for most applications. Perry and Headrick's Pocket Rocket did not even use a stud girdle, let alone two-piece pushrod design!

Chapter 11

The Hybrid Cylinder Head— A Step Beyond

- Exotic hybrid heads
- How to build a true twelve-port six cylinder head
- Advantages of the exotic hybrid head

The term hybrid can be defined as "something of mixed origins or composition." In this instance, it refers to a cylinder head originally made for a different engine, adapted to the Chevy six cylinder block. It may be fit to either the STD-LD or HD-TD series engine.

Why would anyone go to the trouble of adapting a different head to the block? The answer is simple: airflow and inlet runner tuning! While the stock Chevy six head can be made to flow fairly well, it takes extensive work and there are only a handful of shops actively pursuing this head. The stock Siamesed ports have a big disadvantage because they cannot be tuned for optimum runner length—you sacrifice 10–15 percent power and at least that much torque on a naturally aspirated engine!

Imagine that you could solve all of the inherent Chevy six head limitations in one fell swoop: eliminating the nine-port design, wide head bolt spacing, non-cross flow pattern, poor combustion chamber design, high rocker-arm ratio, long pushrod limitations and heavy overall weight.

Along with all these improvements, you could also tap Detroit's best flow experts along with countless shops all

The Anglia of Rydell, Hope and Lang—the first drag car to successfully use a hybrid head on the Chevy six in NHRA national competition.

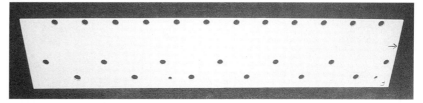
Template for drilling small-block Chevy V8 head bolt pattern into deck of L6 cylinder engine.

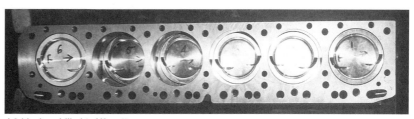
L6 block redrilled to V8 pattern.

Grooved rear oil drainage hole for V8 head (arrow).

After heads are cut, the ends are milled to proper dimensions and V-ed for proper weld penetration.

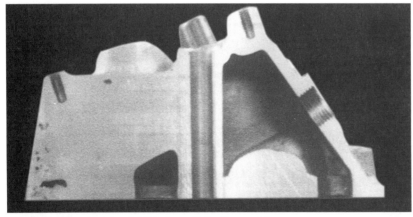

Cut shown through intake port between cylinder three and four.

Heads are mounted to a torque plate for alignment purposes before welding begins. Intake (passenger) side.

across the country, all striving to better the head you were using… perhaps, these thoughts were going through the collective minds of the famous Rydell, Hope and Lang racing team when they conceived the first successful transplant back in 1967. This team went on to set numerous NHRA records with their Anglia drag car and, later, with a Vega funny car.

How successful was this 12-port conversion? Most knowledgeable observers credited the conversion for a .5 second elapsed time advantage over the best prepped stock type head of its day.

Rydell, Hope and Lang used Chevrolet's V8 heads as their basis. Kay Sissell also experimented briefly with the same conversion as well as one made from the Ford Cleveland small block.

NHRA barred the conversions after several seasons. After the rules changed, Kay Sissell went on to pioneer the now famous lump port design using the stock Chevrolet six cylinder head.

Candidates for conversion include:

1. Small-block Chevrolet V8 heads.
2. Chevrolet V6 90 degree heads.

Note: The following two are much more difficult because the valve sequencing is different.

3. Pontiac Iron Duke H.D. four cylinder heads (reborn Chevy II four cylinders).
4. Small-block Ford V8 heads (Cleveland).

This order was determined based on ease of conversion, availability of parts and potential airflow. You might find it odd that the Ford heads are listed last, although they offer proven increases in airflow. The reason is that wide bolt spacing makes for poor combustion sealing qualities. This, along with cooling passage alignment differences, makes this conversion clearly a case of diminishing returns. This is doubly true, now that there are semi-hemi (canted valve) heads for the small-block Chevy V8. When modified, these can flow in excess of 425 CFM at 28" of water.

It should be noted that any of these hybrid conversions require major modification and should not be undertaken lightly.

I will deal with the Chevrolet V8 head conversion which, in my opinion, is the most viable. The areas to be covered include:

1. Block preparation
2. Head selection, dissection, and resurrection
3. Intake manifold
4. Exhaust manifold
5. Cam selection
6. Side covers (lifter gallery)
7. Gaskets
9. Pushrods
10. Distributor

Block Preparation

The block deck surface must be redrilled to accept the V8 bolt pattern. Water passages and oil drain back areas need to be modified.

One of the weak points of using the stock Chevy six head is the four point head bolt arrangement around each cylinder. The V8 uses a much better pentagon shape pattern around each cylinder head (five bolt pattern) which eliminates the need for O-ringing the cylinders. A template can be made by cutting two head gaskets—exactly bisecting the central head bolt hole between cylinders 3 and 4—attaching this to a 1/8" plate and scribing all bolt holes. Drill out all the inscribed holes to proper dimension and, presto, you have

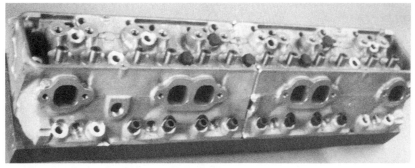

Exhaust side of hybrid aluminum head on torque plate.

Complete L6 aluminum head from Bow Tie Part #14011049—intake side. Note aluminum pieces were cut to fill scalloped cut areas of V8 heads at the gasket face (see prior page).

Deck surface showing welded-in sections that form the intake gasket face.

Close-up showing area between cylinders 2 and 3.

Exhaust side. Note anti-reversion plates.

Top side. Note large diameter springs with titanium retainers.

Chevy Head Selection Chart
(All Measurements are in cc's)

Casting	Port Volume		Combustion Chamber
	Intake	Exhaust	
Street and Strip—Cast Iron			
492 (LT1) #3987376	160	62	64
642 #464045	160	62	73
Oval Track—Cast Iron			
292 (Turbo)	180	62	64
034 (Bow Tie) #10134392	185	55	64
Drags—Aluminum Bow Tie			
049 (Bow Tie) #10051167	175	60	60
101 #10051101	200	65	55
363 HiPort 18° #10134363	210	80	45
363 HiPort 18° CNC#24502482	250	95	50
040 Splayed Valve #10185040	260	95	45
Aftermarket (Brodix, Dart, Airflow Research, Canfield, etc.	230	80	76

Top side of hybrid head.

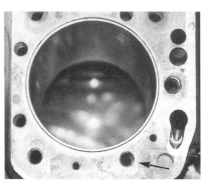

Rear water passage closed using screw-lock method. Compare to photo on page 18. Arrow points to new V8 head bolt hole.

Cast iron L6 head made from "492" castings—intake side. Note epoxy fill-in to form the intake face.

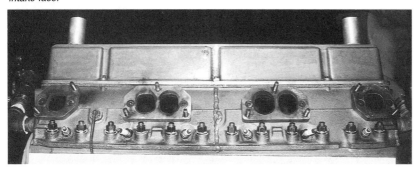

Exhaust side. Note anti-reversion plate fit to exhaust ports and how this spreads the exhaust manifold mounting points. This allows the use of larger diameter headers.

Cast iron Crane "Fireball" head of Gregg Kramer—a project never finished. Note combustion chambers and O-rings.

a plate you can align or a combination template and torque plate can be made by purchasing two Chevy small-block V8 torque plates, sectioning as described above, and rewelding and resurfacing.

Once the pattern is transferred to the six block, drill and tap the deck for the V8 head bolts. Heli-coils can be used for some of the head bolts because they fall directly into the stock Chevy six pattern holes.

The stock deck rear water passage needs to be closed, as one of the V8 head bolts for cylinder number six falls in this opening. See photo page 18. This may be done by brazing in a piece of cast iron or, better, screw-lock in a piece. (A screw-lock kit can be obtained from many automotive machine shops.)

The V8 head oil drainage holes fit approximately where the stock six locating dowels are positioned. A groove needs to be ground from these dowel holes to the adjacent pushrod hole to complete a drainage path. After all work is complete, resurface the deck to ensure a perfect sealing surface.

Head Selection, Dissection, and Resurrection

One interesting coincidence is that the old six cylinder head bolt holes line up very well with the V8 head water passageways. These can be opened up to enhance coolant flow or left as is for short duration events. It's as if Zora Arkus Duntov had imagined some hot rodder might try this combination.

One of the reasons to choose the Chevy V8 head for this conversion is that the block cylinder bores are machined on the same centerline spacing (4.440"). This fact means we really need to make only one cut and weld to make our new hybrid six head.

The selection of head design to use is wide open and largely dependent on your intended usage and pocketbook, because, with current welding technology, the final head may be either cast iron or aluminum. Because this "twelve port" hybrid is a major undertaking, I feel the mildest heads to consider for this project would be the LT-1s (492 casting) even for street use. Choosing a head based on airflow alone would be unwise, because port volume, intake runner configuration and length along with combustion chamber volume (cc's) is equally important. In short, match your

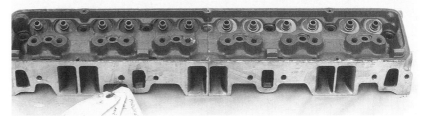

Intake (passenger) side. Note water passages to be closed and scalloping to be filled.

Exhaust (driver) side of head. Note shape of exhaust port—typical of early porting designs.

Head cuts through central bolt hole. Casting must be V-ed for proper weld penetration.

intended usage to available resources. STD-LDs stay with 160-180cc intake volume while HD-TDs can utilize the 180-260cc intake volume.

Making the Cut—Once the head design is chosen, the V8 heads may be sectioned two ways in order to form the six head.

1. Exactly bisect the central head bolt eliminating one cylinder from each head. This cut occurs between the intake ports and forms a three plus three head.
2. Leave one head intact and cut the other between two exhaust ports eliminating two cylinders. This forms a four

plus two combination.

Note: Doing this could create a "hot spot" between exhaust valves. Not a great idea!

I feel the first method is the preferred choice. The V8 heads are put in a mechanical band saw and one cylinder is removed from each head. Remember to cut slightly off center of the bolt hole to leave enough material for milling to final size. A bevel is also cut on each head to provide for better weld penetration.

On the exhaust side of the head, one half of the raised water temperature sending unit base is ground smooth and will be filled in later, during the welding phase.

On the intake side of the

Clifford three 2-barrel Weber manifold modified to fit V8 hybrid L6 head. Note how carburetor linkage is retained for huge Weber 50 DCO carburetors.

Exhaust headers—stepped with long primary pipes and large 3-1/2" collectors. These headers produced terrific low, mid-range and top end power on HD-TD engine.

Clifford four-barrel manifold modified for fuel injection on blow-through turbo engine running methanol.

head, pieces are also cut to fit the various scalloped openings between intake ports. These openings are covered by the V8's intake manifold and are exposed only to the closed lifter gallery whereas on the six cylinder this part of the head overhangs the block and would be open to the air and, therefore must be filled to seal with special wedge shape side covers.

Welding—When all of the pieces are ready, the new head must be mounted to a rigid torque plate or engine block in order to maintain alignment during the welding process. After the top and side portions are welded, the head must be dismounted and turned over for the deck surface to be completed. Once the welding is finished, the deck surface, as well as the intake and exhaust surfaces, must be machine trued. The central bolt hole seat will also need to be trued.

Performance reworking of the head follows standard V8 practices. Remember, treat it like a 400+ CID small block when dealing with the HD-TDs and like a 350 CID when dealing with the 258 CID STD-LDs.

Intake Manifold

Unlimited competition engines can use fuel injection units made for the V8 heads, cut and resectioned to the hybrid. When this is done, the fuel injection pump can fit where the original distributor was located and the distributor moved to the front cover with a special angle drive. Alternatively, you can leave the distributor where it normally is and attach a pump to the timing cover and drive it with the cam shaft. It is also possible to drive the pump from the crankshaft with a Gilmer belt (per Ron's Fuel Injection System design).

Carbureted competition engines should use three, 50 or 55 DCO side draft Webers. These carburetors use a 46mm or 48 mm venturi respectively. A suitable manifold can be made by adapting a Clifford or Sissell six-cylinder manifold. This requires cutting off the six cylinder Siamesed port mounts and replacing them with a 1/2" plate cut to match the V8 head openings. Port dividers must also be fabricated to separate the Siamesed manifold ports. The nice thing about this conversion is that we retain the built-in linkage bars incorporated into the original manifold design.

Dual quad, triple down drafts or single four-barrel designs could also be made from the Clifford six design per above.

Exhaust Manifold

For street use, it may be preferable to cut and weld V8 cast iron dual exhaust headers. For racing, tubular headers, custom made to your chassis, make the most sense. Use the same guidelines suggested in Chapter 12. Tubing, various angle bends and collectors are widely available—remember to purchase the V8 flanges—and six-cylinder collectors.

Cam Selection

General guidelines for cam selection can be found in Chapter 9.

The camshaft can be ground in any configuration—hydraulic, flat tappet or roller tappet. Using Chevrolet V8 heads in this hybrid conversion means we retain the same valve sequencing as originally present in the six cylinder head (E,II,EE,II,EE,II,E).

It should be remembered that the V8 head uses a different ratio rocker arm (1.5 or 1.6) while the six head uses a 1.75 ratio.

Wedge shape side covers—remember the pushrods run outside the block (V8 head is wider than the L6 block). Front cover—outside view.

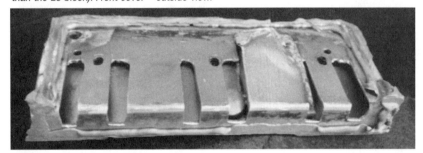

Front cover—block side view.

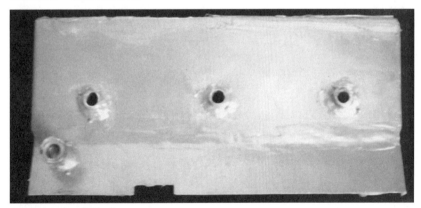

Back cover—outside view.

Back cover—block side view.

```
PART NO: 21F000001
GRIND NUMBER  F-290/400-8          COMPUCAM SPECIAL
ENGINE IDENT.  1963-1984 CHEVROLET L6 CYLINDER 292 CU. IN.
```

VALVE SETTING: INTAKE	.025 16		EXHAUST	.030		→ HOT

		INTAKE @ CAM	400	640	• VALVE 600	ROCKER ARM RATIO
LIFT:		EXHAUST @ CAM	400	640	• VALVE 600	150

ALL LIFTS ARE BASED ON ZERO LASH AND THEORETICAL ROCKER ARM RATIOS

CAM TIMING			OPENS	CLOSES	ADVERTISED DURATION	
@ 020	INTAKE		61° BTDC	87° ABDC	328	°
TAPPET LIFT	EXHAUST		97° BBDC	51° ATDC	328	°

SPRING REQUIREMENTS				RECOMMENDED RPM RANGE WITH MATCHING COMPONENTS	
	TRIPLE	DUAL	OUTER	INNER	
PART NUMBER		99893			MINIMUM RPM
					5000
LOADS CLOSED	120 LBS.	@ 1.875	OR 1-7/8		MAXIMUM RPM
					8000
OPEN	378 LBS.	@ 1.215			VALVE FLOAT
					8000

CAM TIMING		OPENS	CLOSES	MAX LIFT	DURATION
@ 050	INTAKE	42° BTDC	68° ABDC	103° ATDC	290°
TAPPET LIFT	EXHAUST	78° BBDC	32° ATDC	113° BTDC	290°

REMARKS:

Good baseline flat tappet drag cam for HD-TD hybrid head engine.

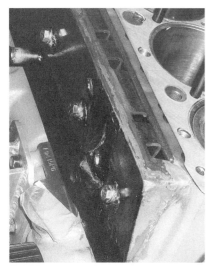

Front cover detail. Note silicone seal.

Front cover detail with head on.

Covers mounted on block—side view.

The lower ratio makes for less valve train stress, although it does reduce the total valve lift.

I have achieved good success when patterning camshaft timing similar to 400 CID Chevy V8 engines (these have similar cubic inch to cylinder volume i.e.: 50 cubic inch per cylinder). What we want to maximize is the six cylinder's inherent low and midrange power, so look for grinds operating in the proper power band when making your selection. Due to the HD-TD's air needs, I would go one step hotter than the recommended grind for a comparable V8.

Side and Valve Covers

Two wedge-shaped side covers must be constructed in order to seal the deck surface of the head and to allow distributor clearance. Remember the pushrods will need clearance so slots will be necessary on the back surfaces of these covers.

The valve cover is a straight-forward sectioning of the two V8 valve covers. Aftermarket covers easily clear big springs and the longer valves of full competition engines.

Gaskets

The head gasket for the hybrid can be hand fabricated of copper or you can cut two V8 gaskets. I have found good success using the HD GM-Fel 020 Teflon® coated composition gasket (GM #14011041). This gasket features a stainless steel O-ring surrounding each cylinder. One cylinder is cut from each gasket to form two three-cylinder gaskets. The actual cut can be made by scribing and cutting with sheet metal shears. This gives a near-perfect cut and match.

With the Teflon® gasket, no sealers are used—but the head

should be retorqued after engine warm up.

I have found the best seal for the side covers, to head and block, to be silicone Ultra Blue no-leak formula by Permatex™. Use a cartridge-size tube and run beads of silicone as needed; trying to use the original six cylinder gaskets has resulted in leaks due to the dissimilar natures of the side cover (steel) and block (cast iron). A valve cover gasket can be made by cutting and siliconing the corresponding V8 gaskets together. Silicone the new gasket to the head and grease the portion that goes against the valve cover so that removing the valve cover is easier. The extra thick Mr. Gasket Ultra Seal #5861 works well.

Pushrods

Pushrods need to be approximately 1.290" shorter than the original six cylinder configuration (another advantage: less flex)—a length of 10.275" OAL provides a starting place but it is essential that you measure and order according to your needs. Moroso makes a pushrod length checker to determine the proper length. The pushrods must be ordered hardened for guide plates. The standard 5/16" diameter is adequate for most applications when ordered with thick wall design (.075") but 3/8" or tapered may be advantageous for ultimate engines.

Distributor

Because the intake manifold is on the ignition side of the block with the hybrid conversion, there is no room for an HEI-sized distributor. Use the early 1963-66 STD-LD small diameter distributor. I further recommend converting this distributor to

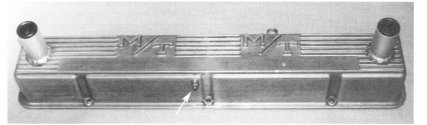

Mickey Thompson small-block Chevy V8 sectioned into L6 valve cover. Note stud to mount Weber accelerator cable.

Corvette small-block Chevy V8 early aluminum covers made into L6 valve cover. Not big enough to clear today's large springs and .100" long valves with roller rockers.

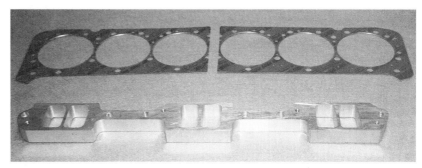

Head gaskets made from Fel-Pro® 8364PT V8 set cut for hybrid L6. Aluminum adapter plate, which was used to modify Clifford four-barrel manifold from L6 port configuration to V8 port configuration.

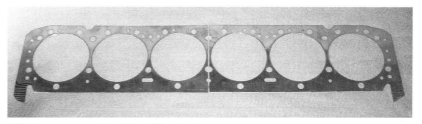

Milodon copper gasket cut from V8 gaskets.

Fel-Pro® gaskets in place on the block. Note Hi Temp silicone on each end of the gasket split (between cylinder 3 & 4). Head is ready to go on.

HD-TD stock head roller cam pushrod vs. hybrid head pushrod (about 1.290" shorter).

Piston design with valve notches for hybrid head. Venolia design 1/16" x 1/16" x 3/16" ring package.

breakerless electronic ignition. This will fit unmodified when used with an HD-TD block. When using an STD-LD block, the distributor must be shortened to provide intake manifold clearance. Remember, the STD-LD block has a 1.75" lower deck height.

Another approach to hybrid power using Mercruiser four cylinder aftermarket heads. The big advantage here is that the bolt pattern for the block deck remains the same. A major disadvantage is virtually no airflow work has been done on these heads. Intake (top) and exhaust (bottom) sides of head.

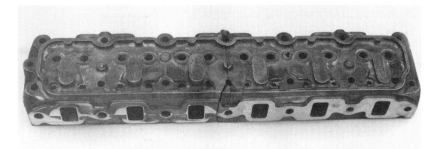

Complete Mercruiser hybrid head prior to welding.

Combustion chamber Mercruiser hybrid head. Note shape and size difference from stock passenger car head.

Chapter 12

Fuel, Exhaust, and Manifolding

- Intake and exhaust systems
- Coordinating selections with engine use
- Specific recommendations to help make a final decision

As you design your Chevy six, eventually you come to handling the incoming fuel and the outgoing exhaust. Thanks again to the engine's original modest performance intent, these are areas where huge improvements can be made over the stock specifications.

This is also an area where having a clear performance goal is important. Your intake and exhaust options are numerous, but some of those options are rather specialized. You don't want to end up with a racing manifold when what you really wanted was a nice running, streetable unit. Having a clear goal for your engine's performance and then sticking to it is important. If you are like most enthusiasts, you'll want a hard-running but reliable street engine that you can take anywhere. In that case, you'll likely end up with a single four-barrel carburetor and either tube headers or one of the better cast iron exhaust manifolds. This chapter will help you decide.

Intake Manifold

The stock HD-TD and STD-LD intake manifolds are for a single carburetor one-barrel design (largest one-barrel carburetor available has a 1-3/4" throttle plate with a 1-5/8" venturi).

Stock HD-TD intake manifold single-barrel, driver side.

Stock HD-TD intake manifold single-barrel, driver side, top.

Stock HD-TD intake manifold single-barrel, bottom.

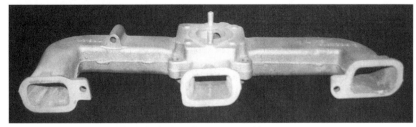

Stock HD-TD intake manifold single-barrel, passenger side.

Offenhauser dual single-barrel manifold with heat box.

Offenhauser triple single-barrel manifold with heat box.

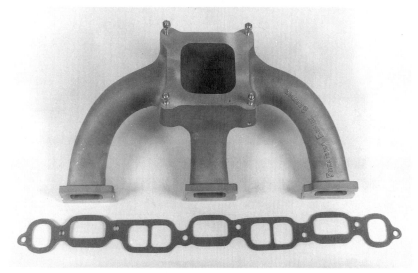

Precision Engine Service Ram four-barrel intake manifold—strictly competition use. Note installed height would be about 17" to 20-1/2" depending on the air cleaner or hat used!

Stock GM two-barrel intake from South America.

Two-barrel adapter for stock intake.

It is attached below the carburetor plenum to the exhaust manifold, typical of Chevy sixes from time immemorial. This attachment is to provide heat to ensure good drivability.

One fact should be immediately evident: This arrangement is meant for only one thing—economy. There is no way an engine of this size can breathe and produce decent horsepower with this restricted arrangement! The minimum that is acceptable, even for street, when using the stock manifold is to use a Clifford Research or Trans-Dapt adapter to mount the Holley large base 350 CFM two-barrel carburetor. You will be pleasantly surprised at the difference this will make, even to a mildly modified engine.

Beyond this level of performance (unless restricted by racing association rules) go to a good aftermarket manifold. Probably the most widely used and easily obtainable, either new or used, is one of the Clifford Research Ram-Flow designs.

Aftermarket

Single Four Barrel—For street/strip, the best choice is a single four-barrel design—available heated or unheated. Heated is an absolute must for street driven cars!

This manifold should be matched with either a Holley 600 CFM vacuum secondary dual feed carburetor or an Edelbrock

600 CFM for optimum results. The STD-LD engine should use a 500 CFM Edelbrock.

A carburetor adapter plate is available from Clifford (Part #08-1013) to convert this manifold into a two-barrel manifold utilizing one of the Holley 350 CFM—600 CFM carburetors (large base). Maximum size recommended for street use is 350 CFM.

Precision Engine Service markets a high performance four-barrel ram design to be used with a bolt-in lump port head. This is strictly a competition manifold with very high runners and is not suitable for street use.

Dual Two Barrel—An alternative to this manifold, for those who like the looks of a dual carburetor setup, and who may anticipate moving up to full competition, is a dual two-barrel manifold (Clifford Part #424501). You would need two base plates (#08-1013) from Clifford. However, remember, in two-barrel form, this is a cosmetic choice—it will not outperform the single four-barrel design and the additional linkage and tuning complications make it less desirable for trouble-free street cruising. A nice combination, based on the dual two-barrel manifold, would utilize Holley staged 350 CFM carbs or Holley-Weber 270 CFM staged carbs.

Dual Four Barrel—The major advantage of the dual two-barrel is that it can be converted into a full competition manifold—dual four-barrel design by changing the carb base plates from Clifford (Part #08-1014—2 required). With this modification and the addition of two Holley 600 CFM four-barrel carbs, this manifold is the poor boy's alternative to the triple Weber side drafts.

Due to the large displacement of the HD-TD, it requires plenty

Clifford Ram Flow intake manifold with two-barrel base plate. These are available with water heat for street use.

Experimental Chevrolet (never released) four-barrel manifold for Quadrajet carburetor.

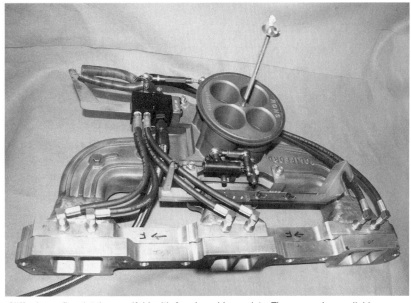

Clifford ram flow intake manifold with four-barrel base plate. These are also available with water heat for street use. This one was adapted to a hybrid head constant flow port injection.

Offenhauser four-barrel manifold—note runner angles—this is a street manifold designed to use the stock cast iron heat riser. Intake port view.

Driver's side view of Offenhauser four-barrel manifold.

Clifford dual-quad intake manifold—with different base plates this can also be a Dual Deuce manifold. This is strictly for competition unless you adapt water heating to the plenums.

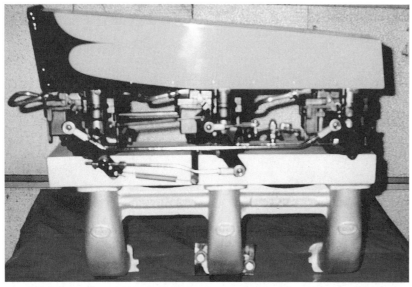

Clifford triple two-barrel high ram manifold—this was originally in tubing and later cast. This example is shown with a homemade plenum connecting all three runners. These are competition manifolds only and were designed for Rochester 2 CG carburetors. With an adapter you can easily fit the large base Holley two-barrel design.

of airflow—more than any single two-barrel or dual two-barrel design can deliver (without expensive and extensive modifications). This is largely due to the fact that single- and two-barrel carburetors are not flowed using the same standard as four-barrel carburetors therefore the net result is that a 600 CFM two-barrel doesn't flow nearly as much as a 600 CFM four-barrel carburetor! It is roughly the equivalent of a 425 CFM four-barrel—if there were such a thing.

The major disadvantage to the dual four-barrel Clifford design is the close carburetor spacing, which prevents the use of Holley dual feed competition four-barrel designs when used inline. Even with this limitation, it is a fine performing manifold. Mounting the carburetors sideways, with the primaries outboard, will provide the needed room to utilize the dual feed designs.

Weber Carbs—For all-out competition, the Clifford/Weber manifold is nearly perfect. This design utilizes mountings for three dual side-draft carburetors. Using this arrangement provides a near perfect flow path from the carbs to the valves.

Weber 45 DCOE model carburetors provide sufficient air/fuel to power all but the most radical engines. (Glen Self's H/MP drag car ran as quick as 10.96 ET/ 123 MPH with this basic setup).

Beyond the 500 horsepower range, special 50 or 55 DCO model carburetors with manifold enlargement and blending are required.

Cotton Perry's H/MP drag car, probably the most powerful HD-TD ever built (10.21 ET/128.11 MPH), ran triple Holley 650 CFM two-barrels on a special dyno-tested, airflowed, custom-built plenum manifold.

Custom plenum manifolds may provide a horsepower advantage for an all-out engine, but be prepared for a geometric increase in cost.

Kay Sissell also marketed a Weber side draft manifold that is on a par with the Clifford design.

Rare Competition Intakes— Over the years, numerous other competition manifolds have been made, usually in the form of triple two-barrel designs. Some of these included:

- Man-A-Fre (made originally for the Pontiac OHC six) but easily adapted to the Chevy six. Due to the very small balance tube between carburetors, without modifications the power potential of this manifold is limited.
- Clifford low-type ram design (similar to the Man-A-Fre).
- Clifford high-type ram design (where underhood space was not a problem).
- Dos Palmos high-type ram design.

If you can locate any of these at a swap meet, they are, when combined with the big Holley 650 CFM two-barrel carbs, on a par with, or slightly superior to, the dual quad manifolds.

Many other manufacturers made various cast manifold configurations over the years. Some of these included Frank's and Offenhauser. Custom-made tube and plenum manifolds are still available from Inline Engine Performance Products, Self Racing Heads & Engines, and Hogan's Racing Manifolds. These plenum manifolds can produce terrific throttle response and top-end horsepower.

Fuel Injection—For competition use, if rules permit, use fuel injection. It not only will permit greater horsepower, but is

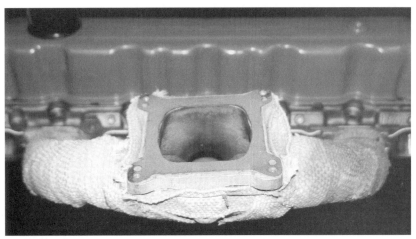

P.E.S. manifold modified for full competition use. Note modifications to the top of the plenum and the insulating wrap on the runners to keep the intake charge cooler.

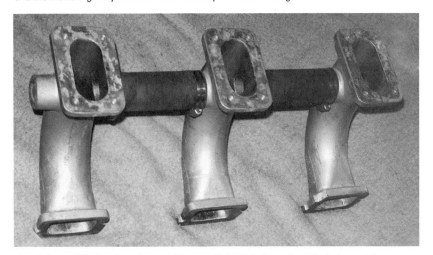

Dos Palmos triple two-barrel competition manifold. Note large diameter balance tubes between the plenums.

Clifford triple side draft Weber intake manifold with Weber 45 DCOE carburetors.

Passenger side view of Glen Self's manifold showing carburetor placement and linkage.

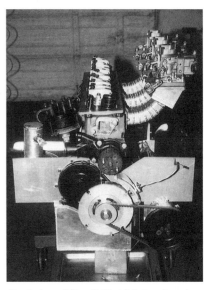

Front view of Glen Self's triple two-barrel competition manifold for STD-LD.

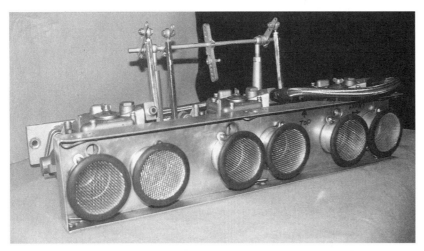

Clifford triple side draft Weber intake manifold enlarged to accept Weber 50 DCO carburetors and adapted for a hybrid head.

Homemade triple two-barrel competition manifold.

easier to convert to alternative fuels such as alcohol or nitromethane.

Fuel injection manifolds were never made commercially in any quantity for the Chevy six. The best known of these commercial units was manufactured by Algon (the design was not noted for its durability or power production). The stock Chevy head design with Siamesed intake ports just cannot take advantage of the manifold tuning normally associated with fuel injection. Mike Kirby at Sissell has developed a mechanical (constant flow) competition injection made to bolt to a Weber manifold that is said to work very well. Electronic fuel injection (computer-aided timed port

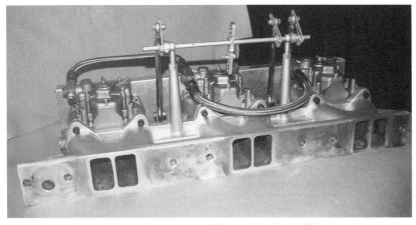

Intake port side view. Note V8 ports and manifold are divided into individual runners.

TRIPLE CARBURETOR MANIFOLD
DESIGNED FOR HIGH RPM, HD-TD

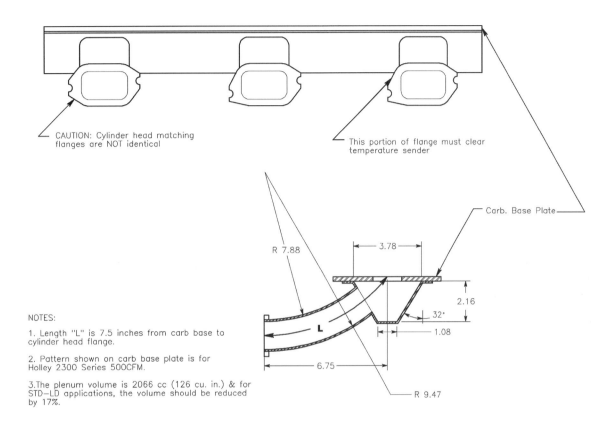

CAUTION: Cylinder head matching flanges are NOT identical

This portion of flange must clear temperature sender

Carb. Base Plate

R 7.88

3.78

2.16

32°

1.08

L

6.75

R 9.47

NOTES:

1. Length "L" is 7.5 inches from carb base to cylinder head flange.

2. Pattern shown on carb base plate is for Holley 2300 Series 500CFM.

3. The plenum volume is 2066 cc (126 cu. in.) & for STD–LD applications, the volume should be reduced by 17%.

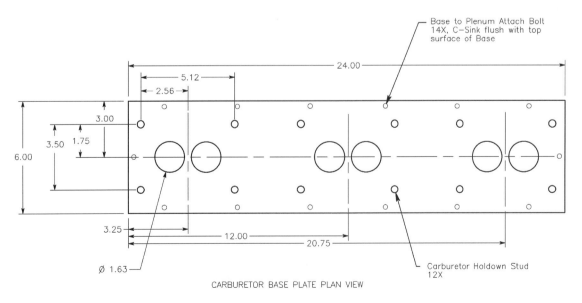

Base to Plenum Attach Bolt 14X, C–Sink flush with top surface of Base

24.00

5.12

2.56

3.00

3.50   1.75

6.00

3.25

12.00

20.75

Ø 1.63

Carburetor Holddown Stud 12X

CARBURETOR BASE PLATE PLAN VIEW

Drawing of port runner and plenum for HD-TD triple two-barrel manifold.

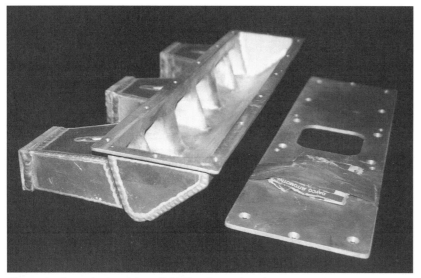

Jerry Haley's homemade cast fuel injection intake manifold, which won him the "Best Engineered" award at the NHRA Spring Nationals in 1965. Note two injectors per port.

Hogan aluminum sheet metal manifold. Note flanges have been removed to convert to hybrid head configuration. Carburetor base plate can be changed to any configuration. This top is cut for a one four-barrel design.

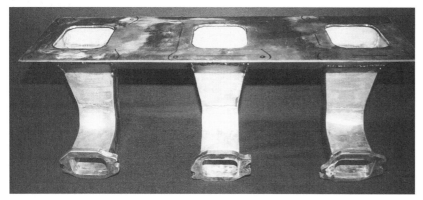

Larry Page's homemade triple four-barrel competition manifold.

Race Engine Design's plenum box for triple two-barrel manifold.

Race Engine Design's triple two-barrel manifold—driver's side. This design combination won more NHRA national events than any other manifold, and was on the Perry and Headrick Pocket Rocket when they won the US Nationals in 1981.

Race Engine Design's triple two-barrel manifold—back view.

injection) will be available soon, but the cost is likely to be a stumbling block to widespread use. Clifford Research also markets a throttle-body fuel injection for the single four-barrel manifolds. This manifold is intended primarily for street use. General Motors of Mexico makes a two-barrel throttle body fuel injection system for the STD-LD truck applications that may be adapted to street driven cars. Holley Pro-Jection® four-barrel digital fuel injection could also be easily adapted to six-cylinder use atop a Clifford four-barrel manifold.

The most successful competition fuel injection on a Chevy six probably was Jerry Haley's (Rockford, Illinois) meticulous custom-made unit, which won him the "Best Engineered" award at the NHRA Spring Nationals in 1965. Many other examples of custom-made injection exist such as Harry Blecha's gas coupe and David Jones' front engine nostalgia dragster, both HD-TDs.

It is possible to adapt a small-block Chevy V8 fuel injection set up to the six cylinder head by cutting off the V8 flanges and welding on a 1/2" aluminum plate patterned and spaced to fit the six-cylinder ports. A further alternative might be to build a custom plenum ram manifold and utilize an Hilborn hat-type of fuel injection such as on Jim Tinsmith's beautiful HD-TD nostalgia altered. A Ron's Fuel Injection 4-shooter or Flying Toilet on a Clifford four-barrel manifold would also work very well with minimal effort.

Exhaust Manifold

The 1969 and later stock HD-TD exhaust manifold is a straight-forward cast iron affair, with some incorporating a heat riser valve below the attachment to the

Man-A-Fre triple two-barrel intake manifold—used Rochester 2CG carburetors, can be adapted to Chevy. The balance tube between plenums proved too small.

Frank Pattern and Manufacturing single four-barrel intake manifold—used AFB carburetor.

Frank Pattern and Manufacturing dual four-barrel intake manifold—used WCFB carburetors.

David Jones' homemade cast fuel injection intake manifold built by Steve Richard. Hilborn components and pump. Note large diameter of throttle plates and single injector per port.

Jim Tinsmith's homemade tubular fuel injection intake manifold with plenum utilizing Hilborn V8 hat-type throttle bodies. Note single injector per port.

Harry Blecha's homemade fuel injection manifold utilizing Hilborn components and pump. The 2-9/16" diameter throttle plates are fed by 10" ram tubes—a single injector per port is used.

Chevrolet experimental cast iron dual exhaust manifolds (circa 1965)—never released.

intake plenum. Its shape tends to mimic the (194-250) STD-LD manifolds with most having a center exhaust exit. Earlier HD-TD manifolds (1963–1968) are more streamlined and have no heat riser valve but do provide some passive flow to the intake. Their rear exhaust exit tends to interfere with the chassis when adapted to some passenger cars and may also interfere with the clutch linkage on some trucks. However, this manifold does feature larger passages and incorporates provisions for a significantly larger exhaust head pipe (2-1/2 inches) and features a 3-bolt flange, where the STD-LD manifolds have a 2-bolt flange.

When the stock-type exhaust manifold must be retained, it is worth investing in a custom head pipe to utilize the HD-TD manifold on the STD-LD block series engine for street use.

For high performance street use, classic look cast iron headers are available from Langdon's Stovebolt Engine Parts Company. These headers are available plain or Thermo-barrier ceramic coated and they fit both the STD-LD blocks and the HD-TD engines. Kansas Kustoms can also modify your manifold for dual exhaust as a less expensive alternative.

Tubular Headers

Racing applications should use tubular headers appropriate for their chassis and engine modification level.

Cylinders 1, 2, 3 are tied together into a cloverleaf collector and then into an extension or outlet pipe. Cylinders 4, 5, 6 should be a duplicate system. Complete headers, as well as header flanges, U-bends, collectors, etc., are available from a number of sources including Clifford Research.

Langdon's Stovebolt later-design cast iron dual exhaust manifolds (2-bolt flanges). These have recently been redesigned to eliminate interference with the motor mount and clutch linkage.

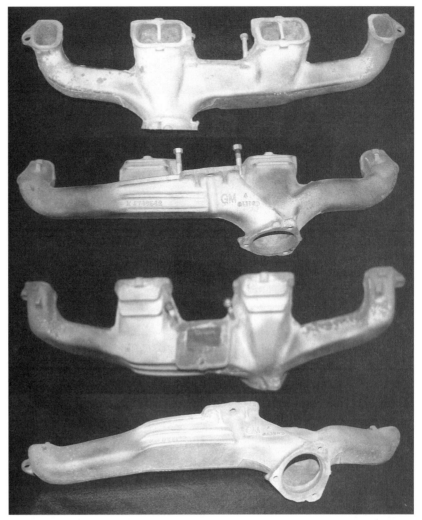

Stock cast iron HD-TD exhaust manifold. Note rear exit for head pipe, 3-bolt flange and large 2-1/2" diameter opening.

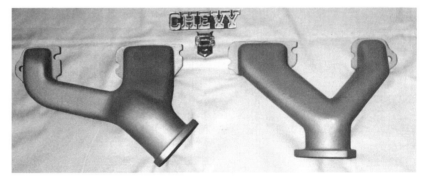

Langdon's Stovebolt early-design cast iron dual exhaust manifolds (3-bolt flanges). These fit both HD-TD and STD-LD engine series. This is an excellent choice for any street application. Be prepared to modify motor mount and clutch linkage to avoid exhaust interference.

Some important points to remember:

1. It is better to err in favor of smaller pipe sizes rather than larger—bigger is usually not better. Use 1-7/8"–2" only for the most radical HD-TD engines. STD-LDs may use up to 1-3/4" when dressed out in a similar fashion. For drag cars, this means engines producing enough power to run 11.30s in HD-TD form and 11.80s in STD-LD form in the quarter-mile. Some racers use a step-type header to preserve maximum exhaust velocity at the port.

2. Automatic transmission-equipped cars need longer primary pipes, collectors and extensions to broaden the torque curve. Collector lengths as long as 36 inches can be beneficial for mid-range torque without sacrificing peak power.

3. Never use the stock manifold for anything beyond street use. It is not compatible with racing cams because of their high overlap.

4. To provide the classic "split-six" sound, for a street driven car, no balance tube should be used between collectors. To achieve the old-fashioned "rapping" sound when you decelerate, mount the mufflers closer to the collectors and use two-inch diameter tail pipes all the way to the rear bumper. Mufflers should be glasspacks or steelpacks with a round hole perforated core design (not louvered-core type). These mufflers are usually sized 18"–24". Beware of reproductions. Many have louvered core inside.

Exhaust Header Specifications

	Primary Pipe O.D.	Primary Pipe Length	Collector	Crossover	Notes
Street/Strip	1-5/8"	36-38"	6 x 2-1/2" cloverleaf	1-5/8"	Max perf. w/ reasonable sound
Strip	1-3/4"	36-38"	6 x 2-1/2" cloverleaf	none	2-1/2" x 12-24" extensions
Super Strip	1-7/8 or 2"	34-36"	6 x 3-1/2" cloverleaf	none	3-1/2" x 6-12" extensions

Notes: Street/Strip exhaust system should use 2-1/2" exhaust tubing and two "turbo" mufflers. Omit crossover pipe if classic rapping six cylinder sound is desired. Extension length on Strip and Super Strip systems is ultimately determined by trial and error. Start with longer pipe and cut off 2" sections until maximum performance is obtained. Optional megaphones may improve ET as much as .05 second. Megaphones should slowly expand outward from the collector to a length of 36".

Zoomie headers can be used on lightweight cars with big CID engines successfully. This example is David Watkins' blown HD-TD roadster. Most cars are better off with collector-style headers.

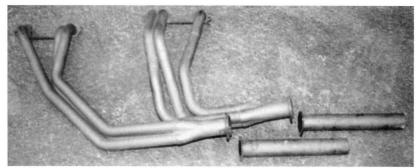

Tubular headers for a drag car—Clifford research—1-3/4" diameter x 36" length with 6-1/2" x 2-1/2" collectors. Collector extensions of 16-1/2" worked well on both STD-LD and HD-TD engines in a car of 2700 pounds or more.

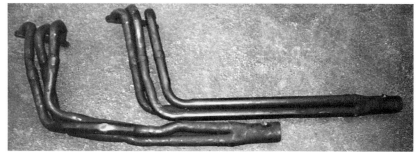

Custom-made step headers for hybrid head HD-TD drag car. Note long primary pipes and large 3-1/2" diameter x 9-1/2" collectors.

Oval track crossover tubular headers for STD-LD featuring 1-1/2" diameter x 42" length with 7" x 2-7/8" collectors.

Chapter 13

Ignition—Lighting the Fire for Power

- Distributor ignitions, advance curves
- Magnetos and crank triggered ignitions
- Coils and Wires
- Spark plugs and gaps

One of the best things about running Chevrolet is the amazing parts interchangeability between various years. This fact is very evident when it comes to distributors. You can literally bolt in any six-cylinder unit from the late 1940s on up. The advantage is that you can choose from many fine units at reasonable costs.

Distributor

Early distributors have a different mounting arrangement but as long as you use the early-style clamp it will work in the HD-TD with very little modification—even the gear is the same! One cautionary note—the pre-1954 distributors used a steel gear that is not compatible with post-1954 cast iron camshafts. Be sure to change this with a later gear if using one of these older distributors in a later engine. Why bother with a 20+ year old distributor? Mallory made a fine dual-point conversion kit for the pre-1962 units and it is capable of 7000+ RPM easily. Many of these units can be found at swap meets.

Another good unit is the Mallory distributor featuring dual points, 3-lobe cam design, external condenser and made in

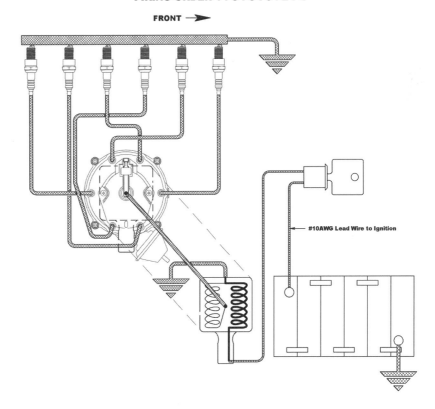

HEI WITH INTEGRATED COIL IGNITION
FIRING ORDER 1 . 5 . 3 . 6 . 2 . 4

FRONT ➡

#10AWG Lead Wire to Ignition

HEI diagram with integrated coil ignition. Twelve volt battery power. Firing order 1,5,3,6,2,4.

large quantities from the 1950s on up. This unit will fire a competition engine at 7,000+ with a stock Chevy coil! Points, condensers, cap and rotors are still available.

The stock Chevy distributors

made from 1963 up until the introduction of the HEI (High Energy Ignition) also respond well to electronic conversion kits, high performance point sets, external condenser, etc.

You may also wish to

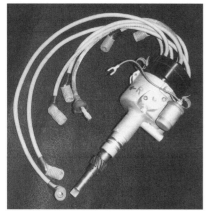

Early-style Mallory 235-261 CID distributor. Note clamp style of mounting and O-ring to prevent oil leakage.

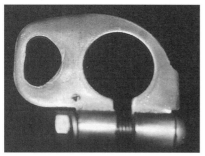

Clamp for early distributors.

1963–74 Chevy six single-point distributor. Note collar for mounting instead of early-style clamp.

Mallory dual point conversion for early distributor with external condenser attached.

through multi-stage rev limiters all the way up to laptop computer control, these systems can fit the need.

HEI ignition

The array of performance distributors became complete in 1975 with the introduction of the HEI for the Chevy six. This unit utilizes a magnetic pickup assembly and is an excellent unit capable of firing in excess of the HD-TD's RPM capability. Those units made in 1975–76 were unique. They had a separate coil and better cap orientation and are preferred by many racers and street rodders, due to their enhanced spark plug wire appearance.

If you choose to use the HEI, remember to use only solid core spark plug wires for racing applications. An adequate gauge ignition lead to the distributor is a must. A #10 lead wire is required with no other electrical components drawing voltage off the ignition switch. Use separate switches for electric water pump, fuel pump, etc. For full competition engines, eliminate the vacuum advance mechanism. For street use, a good quality spiral core spark plug wire set is needed to eliminate radio interference.

You should be getting the feeling by now that finding a good ignition is not a problem for the Chevy six. Any competent ignition shop can set up any one of the above units and you will be ready for bear when combined with the proper wires, coil and spark plugs.

Advance curve

For street/mild strip use, an advance curve with 10 degrees initial lead with full advance in at 3000 RPM. On a street engine with a "hot" camshaft, the engine

eliminate the mechanical advance mechanism (weights and springs) and go electronic with something like MSD's fixed or programmable timing computers. The advantages are numerous with a modern electronically-controlled capacitive discharge ignition like the MSD, Crane and others. Multi spark strikes per ignition event at low RPM give an amazingly smooth idle and more rapid throttle response right off idle, plus there is no end to the add-on accessories supported by these ignitions. From simple boost and nitrous retards may run better at idle with full vacuum to the vacuum canister thus giving a total advance at idle of 30° (10° initial + 20° vacuum).

Racing applications use an advance curve with 10 degrees initial lead with full advance in at 2000 RPM.

Total timing will vary depending on many factors and experimentation will be the final guide. Generally though, it will fall between 32–38 degrees.

Magnetos

Magnetos have been used on some of the fastest Chevy sixes ever built—going all the way back to the Wayne Horning 12-port head conversions and "California Bill" Fisher up to Glen Self's record-holding HD-TD H/MP Camaro.

The major advantage of a magneto is that it creates its own voltage through a built-in generator—the higher the RPM of the engine the hotter the spark generated. The whole unit is compactly packaged and replaces the distributor and utilizes the same cam drive mechanism as the stock distributor. Although magnetos work well for racing, they have low voltage output at low speeds, so they are not good for street applications.

For bracket racing, the magneto's self-generating capability can be a big advantage where there are lots of electrical demands (fuel pump, water pump, cooling fans, etc.) and reliability is a must. With the magneto, you won't have to carry the weight of extra batteries or have to frantically charge batteries between rounds to ensure adequate ignition voltage!

One word of caution: Do not use a magneto with any type of stutter box or retard as the resulting pulsing has been known to break camshafts! Also, a magneto will not allow the many

Mallory dual point distributor—3-lobe design. Note provision for mechanical tachometer drive and external condenser missing.

Distributor modified to lock out vacuum advance. Note large external condenser.

Shims between the distributor gear and housing are not critical because this is a down-thrust distributor.

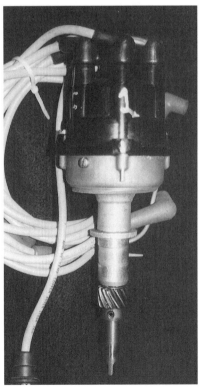

For steel billet roller cams, change the gear to a bronze style.

electronic delay boxes and other ignition accessories that are so popular today.

The most common units made for the Chevy/GMC six were, and still are, made by Vertex. Spalding and Barker-Wico also made units in the '50s—remember the interchangeability that we discussed earlier.

The big disadvantage to the magnetos is the initial cost—unless you can find one at a swap

Pre-HEI distributor modified to eliminate points with a Crane optical XR-700 electronics unit.

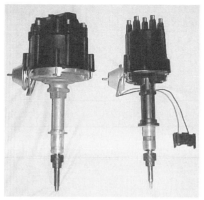

Integral coil HEI compared for size with Langdon's Stovebolt nostalgia HEI distributor using a separate coil.

Distributor Pad Machining

Many 250 CID engines wore out the lower distributor bushing due to an inaccurately machined mounting pad for the distributor "collar." The pad was not machined perpendicular to the axis of the distributor bore, so when the hold down clamp was tightened, it twisted the distributor out of alignment. Always check this pad for squareness and remachine if necessary, or you will risk wearing out your "new" distributor. It is also possible to use a shim under one side of the distributor collar instead of machining.

At right is pre-HEI distributor advance curve altered by replacing original springs with lighter V8 springs—all advance in at 3000 RPM.

meet at the right price, it is far more cost-effective to build one of the distributors for most applications.

Although it has been reputed that a magneto will produce more horsepower, dyno tests have demonstrated no horsepower advantage with a magneto versus HEI ignition. I have never been able to demonstrate any ET reduction in my bracket car.

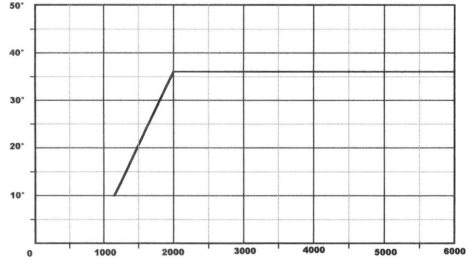

Graph of a typical competition spark advance curve.

Cotton Perry's *Pocket Rocket*—probably the fastest HD-TD H/MP ever built—claimed to go faster by a tenth of a second using a Unilite electronic Mallory distributor over his tried and true Vertex magneto.

Coils

For HEI distributors, the stock components are usually adequate. An MSD conversion unit plus special coil further enhance this already fine distributor.

The Mallory 3-lobe, dual point distributor works well with stock Chevy coil.

The dual point conversion kit for early distributors works best with a heavy-duty aftermarket coil (take your pick: Mallory, Accel, MSD, etc.) The electronic conversion kits—Unilite, Petronix, Crane—all work well with the stock Chevy coil.

I have run an early distributor (1965) with a single-point set and external Mallory condenser (with stock coil) on my HD-TD bracket car and have gone as quick as 11.18 and 115+ in the quarter mile.

Spark Plug Wiring

Any aftermarket solid core (metallic) wiring works well with distributors or magnetos, just be sure to use wire separators to prevent crossfire.

The HEI uses a heavier gauge plug wire; again use only solid core wire (metallic) when racing.

Spark Plugs

The Chevy six is not a hard engine on plugs. The standard plug in the later heads is a 14mm taper seat 5/8" Hex type. Pre-1970 heads used a 14mm gasketed plug with 3/4" reach—13/16" hex type.

For street use only, you may

Early HEI distributor featuring separate coil.

Late HEI distributor with integral coil.

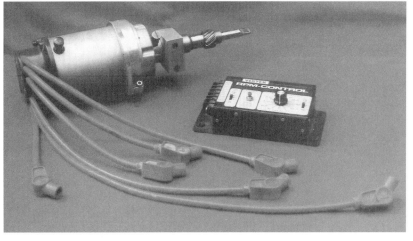

A magneto can be a good alternative for a bracket car, as it generates its own spark.

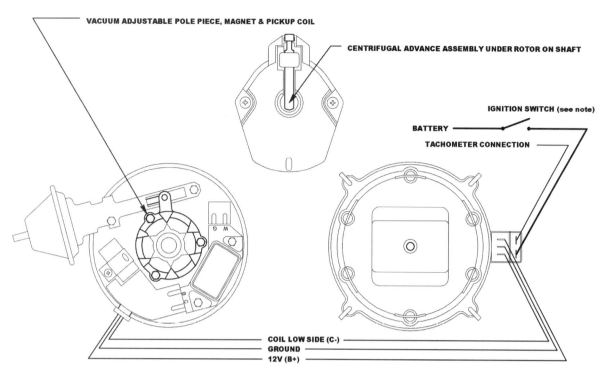

VACUUM ADJUSTABLE POLE PIECE, MAGNET & PICKUP COIL

CENTRIFUGAL ADVANCE ASSEMBLY UNDER ROTOR ON SHAFT

IGNITION SWITCH (see note)

BATTERY

TACHOMETER CONNECTION

COIL LOW SIDE (C-)
GROUND
12V (B+)

HEI DISTRIBUTOR

NOTE: Separate #10AWG circuit required for ignition switch not shared by any other accessories

HEI distributor and rotor cut-away.

Crank-triggered ignition in STD-LD. Note sensor positions moved to 120° apart (as opposed to V8 positions at 90° apart).

wish to run a resistor plug. For all other applications, use the regular style.

Plug Gaps

Plug gap for dual point distributor ignition is .028". With MSD conversions or HEI, wider gaps of .050"–.080" may be used. The wider gap may enhance idle quality for street driven vehicles. For magnetos, use only a .015" gap. (This is a reflection of how weak the spark is at cranking speed—150 RPM.)

Chapter 14

Supercharging—
When Enough Isn't Enough

- Selecting the correct "Roots" blower
- Camshaft and carburetion
- Intercoolers
- The latest centrifugal superchargers

When you've bored, stroked, increased the compression, maximized the airflow, injected the maximum amount of fuel, played with nitrous oxide, and maybe even gone a step further and switched from gasoline to alcohol or something really exotic like nitromethane, and you're still yearning for more power—then it's time to raise the ante! Sometimes even Mother Nature needs a boost, so when atmospheric pressure isn't doing the job, we need to find a mechanical way to put even more air and fuel through that engine—literally to pack it in! Phenomenal increases in horsepower can be obtained by supercharging or turbocharging. Both methods lead to similar horsepower.

In this chapter we'll start our examination of forced induction by taking a look at supercharging. Our inline sixes make ideal candidates, because they already have strong lower ends and very good factory oiling systems. In essence, what we are up to is using a mechanical crank-driven compressor to force greater volumetric efficiency. We want to get more fuel and air into our engine than atmospheric pressure alone can supply.

Blower Types—Traditionally the most common supercharger

Walt Skoczylas' 1932 Bantam—6-71 blown HD-TD.

design has been the Roots-type, exemplified by the GMC 4-71 and 6-71 models. These blowers, or huffers, as they are called, are the ones like we've seen on dragsters since Don Garlits pioneered their use in the late '50s with his famous *Swamp Rat* slingshot dragster.

Another type of supercharger that merits close attention is a new generation of centrifugal blower exemplified by the Pro Charger by Accessible Technologies, Inc. We'll talk more about this type after a full

discussion of the Roots blower application.

Of course, our first thought is for full competition use, but there is another place where superchargers make sense—the street rod.

For instance, supercharging would allow you to run a very mild stock HD-TD long block with only a cam change and— poof—you have a mean sounding, smooth running powerhouse with excellent reliability—at a very modest cost.

Let's look at some specific tips

California Bill—Roots blower installation on a 1950 Chevrolet. Note side-draft carburetors and cool air intake.

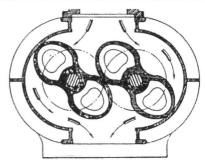

Cross-section of Roots-type supercharger. Arrows indicate direction of airflow.

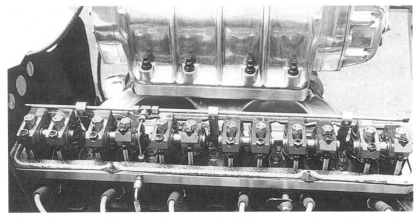

Stovebolt intake manifold—originally designed for B&M blowers. An adapter plate is made to put on the 4-71 or 6-71. This is made of 1-1/2" thick aluminum.

Cross-section of a centrifugal supercharger—arrow indicates direction of airflow.

Dave Watkins' 1934 Chevy Roadster— 6-71 blown HD-TD with dual Holley Dominator carburetion.

on what we do once we have decided to pursue the use of a blower.

Which Blower to Use?

First, you need to be aware that Roots blowers (3-71, 4-71, 6-71, 8-71, 10-71 and 14-71) are made for diesel use by GM and must be converted in order to be used for an automotive application. The 8-71, 10-71 and 14-71 blowers are really not practical unless you use an aftermarket version due to the mounting arrangement and bolt pattern of the original GM units. Internal modifications have to be made to the other three preferred blowers for automotive

use, so if you're contemplating a used unit, at a swap meet, remove the rear bearing cover and be sure it contains the correct bearing (6205-2RS), or you'll be in for expensive conversion costs!

The 3-71 and 4-71 models use a 4-bolt pattern while the 6-71 and larger use an 8-bolt pattern. For 99 percent of all applications you will want either a 4-71 or 6-71 model. These blowers have a long history of reliability and should be your first choice. Weiand also makes an excellent new blower (model #1604), which is available both polished and unpolished and is another possibility.

Avoid V-series GM blowers, as well as the Eaton V6 GM blower now used on current front-wheel drive Buicks and Pontiacs. (The snout is too short for our use.) We also avoid other new blowers, as they have not been as reliable as our preferred models.

To my knowledge, there is currently no commercially cast blower intake manifold for Chevy inline engines. Inline Engine

Performance Products can custom make a blower manifold for you. Blown Plum Crazy can modify a Clifford four-barrel manifold for blower use.

Crank drive pulleys and Gilmer drive belt, brackets, etc., are all readily available separately or as a complete kit.

Compression Ratios

Keep the static compression ratio in the range of 7.5 to 8.5 to 1, unless you are building the engine strictly as a trailered to the track competition engine. These compression ratios are obtained with custom dished pistons made specifically for blower applications and are available from most piston manufacturers. Cast pistons are not recommended except for street use with very low boost applications (4 to 6 lbs.). Forged pistons are easily the best choice for most engines. Use slotted skirts for street use and solid skirt design for competition.

When determining the proper ratio to use, you must take into account the weight of the car, gear ratios, tire sizes and your intended use—street cruising, towing a trailer, etc. Quality of gasoline is also an important factor. Supercharged engines are extremely sensitive to detonation. In short, it is better to err on the side of less compression ratio than more compression ratio. It is much easier to speed up the blower with a pulley change than to have to tear the engine down and replace the pistons. Maximum power will be achieved with a lower compression ratio and more boost—even with racing engines!

Camshafts

A wide variety of camshafts are available from most cam companies. A full discussion

As a tightly sealed racing Roots blower can drain 100+HP through a tightly tensioned drive belt, bearing wear on the upper half of the number one main bearing, not to mention bending forces on the crankshaft, are an issue. A good solution is to fabricate a crankshaft support similar to this one.

On a lightweight drag car, the blower on an HD-TD engine would be underdriven anywhere between 10–40 percent depending on the power band of the camshaft. This is altered by the pulley sizes.

Crower eight port fuel injection system is used on top of Walt Skoczylas' 6-71 blown HD-TD engine.

about your specific application should take place before you plunk down the cash.

Competition Cams has a Cam Helpline with knowledgeable people who know blower engine requirements. Also, Isky Cams has been active with blown engines for years. (Remember those Ohio George (Isky) vs. Stone, Woods and Cook (Engle) supercharged coupe wars of the '60s? Isky would spot them 100 cubic inches and still rule!)

Two 1150 CFM Holley Dominator carburetors are used on Dave Watkins' 6-71 blown HD-TD engine.

Header design features three into one collectors on Skoczylas' 1932 Bantam.

Dave Watkins uses six individual zoomie exhaust pipes on his 1934 Chevy roadster.

Camshaft Selection Chart

Street—Hydraulic Lifters

Duration at .050"	Lift	Lobe Center Line
STD-LD engines		
218°	.460"	110°
224°	.470"	110°
HD-TD engines		
238°	.460"	110°

Competition—Solid or Roller Lifters

Full bodied cars

Duration	Lift	Lobe Center Line
242°	.550"	110°

Dragster/Altered (1500 lbs. and under)

272° Intake	.735"	110°
280° Exhaust	.735"	110°

duration as an unblown engine, and that the larger the engine, the more tolerant of duration it will be, blown or not. A 194 CID engine will not run well with a cam designed for a 292 CID engine.

Furthermore, going to a wider lobe center, i.e., 114 degrees, is *not* recommended. While it will build more cylinder pressure, it will also build more heat and geometrically increases the chance of detonation. On the other hand, too close a lobe center increases the valve overlap. If this is overdone the blower will fan some of the incoming air/fuel mixture right down the exhaust port because the intake and exhaust valves will be open for a relatively long time together. Stick close to standard naturally aspirated lobe center values.

Drive Belt

For typical street use, a half inch pitch or 8mm pitch (if you would like a quieter drive) is suggested. For competition use with alcohol as a fuel, a 13.90mm or 14mm drive ratio is suggested. There are charts to match each

The people at Delta Camshafts have been very helpful and are knowledgeable about inline engines used in blower applications as well.

Here are some specific grinds that work: (Durations are at .050" lifter rise—advertised durations will appear much greater).

Remember that a blown engine does not need nearly the

ATI carburetor bonnet.

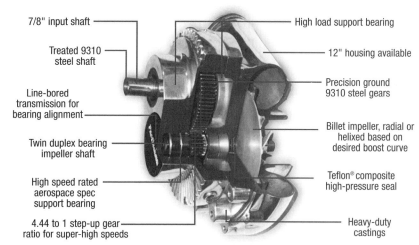

- 7/8" input shaft
- Treated 9310 steel shaft
- Line-bored transmission for bearing alignment
- Twin duplex bearing impeller shaft
- High speed rated aerospace spec support bearing
- 4.44 to 1 step-up gear ratio for super-high speeds
- High load support bearing
- 12" housing available
- Precision ground 9310 steel gears
- Billet impeller, radial or helixed based on desired boost curve
- Teflon® composite high-pressure seal
- Heavy-duty castings

Any of the centrifugal blowers could be easily adapted to either the STD-LD or HD-TD engines with the bonus of adding an intercooler for added horsepower. This cutaway illustrates the ATI blower internals, which are typical of the modern crop of centrifugals.

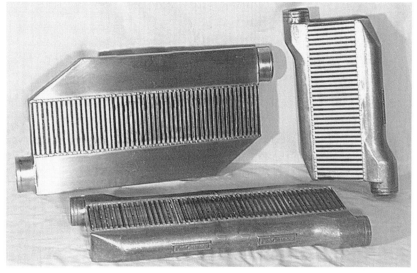

ATI intercoolers.

car for intended use, weight, compression ratio, cubic inch and pounds of boost desired. Typically, for a street-driven engine, you want to underdrive the blower 9–10 percent less than the speed of the crankshaft.

Carburetion and Fuel Injection

Superchargers present an interesting dilemma. When you're cruising at low speeds, it's like any other normally aspirated motor—but, when you step on it, the airflow requirements build geometrically! So, what we are looking for is a carburetor that acts like a small carb (small primaries), but can provide a smooth transition to high flow conditions (large secondaries).

Adjustment can best be made with vacuum secondaries or with mechanical secondaries with vacuum operated flaps (as in a Carter Competition design). Carter or Edelbrock version of the AFB, as well as the Predator, will bolt on and go—adjust if necessary. Holley's must be dialed in for blower use; don't even try them without doing so!

Mechanical (non-timed) constant flow fuel injection works very well with blowers, but only for competition engines. Do not attempt to use it on the street. Many of the older V8 blower injection units, while not up to today's standard for full competition V8 engines, work very well for our inline engines. Any used unit must be flowed

and calibrated before installation. Consult any injection specialist for advice and service. Kinsler is a good source.

Fully timed computer controlled injection would work well on the street, but the cost of a custom system is prohibitive for most enthusiasts.

Ignition Timing

Because detonation must be avoided, you should sneak up on ignition timing. Initial advance will be between 12 to 20 degrees—start with 16. Total advance usually falls in the

28–32 degree range with all centrifugal advance in by 3,000 to 3,400 RPM. New or used distributors must be tested and advance curve set. Use a dual vacuum advance pressure retard canister. Alternatively, you can use an MSD timing computer and fix the advance plate solidly in the distributor.

In non-HEI distributors, it is the ideal time to upgrade and do away with ignition points by converting to optical or magnetic triggers. These are available from Crane/Allison or Petronix or take the opportunity to convert to an HEI unit.

Vortech waste gate.

Vortech carburetor enclosure.

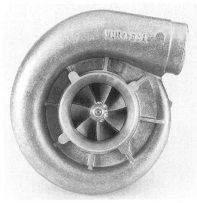

Vortech centrifugal superchargers—various models available.

ATI Procharger centrifugal superchargers—various models available.

Fuel Requirements

Unleaded fuel is okay for the street, but the "final compression ratio" of the motor/blower combination is the determining factor in the octane requirements. If you plan to run 87 octane fuel (regular unleaded), forget about supercharging! With 92 octane (premium street fuel), go no more than 7.5 to 1 on the ratio. With full competition engines, do not exceed 10 to 1, even with alcohol. A very potent competition engine can be made with 8 to 1 compression and the right combination of pulleys to create the necessary boost.

A final word of caution: Detonation is sudden death to a supercharged motor—period!

Intercooling, though difficult with a Roots blower, can add increased life to an engine, as well as add about 30 percent more power. Remember, a blower can easily raise the inlet charge temperature to well over 250°F simply in the process of compressing the air. Whether intercooled or not, all street engines need knock sensors with timing retard features (available from MSD) to protect the engine from detonation. These work much better than the old water injection or vapor methods for controlling detonation.

The case for using a Roots blower despite its propensity to heat the incoming air is that it is able to provide boost (positive displacement) right from idle, unlike centrifugal and turbo chargers, which work by pure fluid momentum. This instant boost means instant throttle response at virtually any RPM— a very desirable characteristic for any street-driven vehicle!

Decide what you want before you build the motor and stick to it. Educate yourself by reading everything you can on the subject. This chapter just touches on the highlights. Car Tech/SA Design Publishing has two must-read books about Roots supercharging. They are: *Super Power* by Larry Schreib and *Street Supercharging* by Pat Ganahl.

Centrifugal Superchargers

There are several important reasons to consider a centrifugal supercharger over a Roots supercharger system:

1. It is a much more efficient way of compressing air and producing boost. Less horsepower drain off the crankshaft = more horsepower at the rear wheels.
2. It has a greater adiabatic efficiency thus heats the air less when compressing the incoming charge and lends itself to the use of an intercooler. This automatically makes it possible to produce up to an additional 30 percent more horsepower with less chance of detonation.
3. Due to its compact size, it is an easier unit to adapt to inline engines requiring no additional hood clearance and it blows into an easily obtainable four-barrel intake manifold.
4. Modified carburetors, drive systems and air delivery tubes are easily adapted from V8 kits.

If you are thinking of super-charging, this new generation of centrifugal units may be the way to go—for street-driven vehicles and race cars.

Companies that are at the forefront of centrifugal super-charging are Accessible Technologies, Inc.(ATI), Vortech, Paxton and Powerdyne™.

Chapter 15

Turbocharging— A Different Route

- Taking the mystery out of adiabatic efficiency
- Draw-through and blow-through turbo systems

"If turbocharging you have tried, surely a piston you have fried."
— Ak Miller, 1960

With a close reading of this chapter and study on your part, maybe we can relegate this quote to ancient history.

Ak Miller is considered by many to be the Godfather of hot rod turbocharging. After getting off the phone with him, you ask yourself if you have been living in some other world. You wonder how you could possibly have missed, or dismissed, turbocharging when, indeed, it comes as close to a perfect way to add power to an engine as there is! What it can give you is significant horsepower without causing the RPM range to get out of hand (above 6,000).

Inline engines are known for their torque—they are not RPM machines. Does anyone see a natural match here? All of this leads me to conclude that turbocharging is probably the most misunderstood, unappreciated and underutilized way of building inline power.

Adiabatic Efficiency

There is one thing that separates Roots superchargers from turbochargers and that is adiabatic efficiency. As Ak says, "You never

Bob Brown's 1937 Chevy Coupe—turbo HD-TD powered street rod.

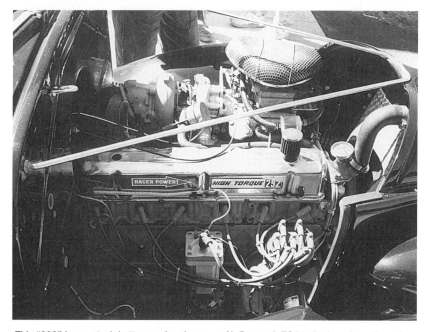
This "292" has a stock bottom end and uses an Air Research TO4 turbo in a draw-through system. A Holley 600 CFM vacuum secondary four-barrel completes the package.

TO4 utilizes an integral waste gate, which greatly simplifies turbo plumbing in a street rod.

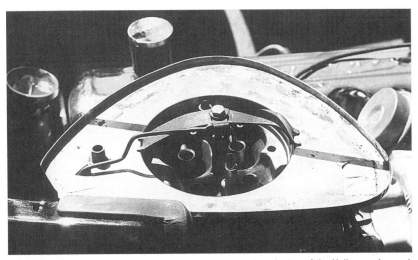

Water injection is hooked to a Hobbs switch and sprays into the top of the Holley on demand. Windshield washer fluid is used to suppress detonation. Spray begins at 4 pounds of boost.

Water-heated carb plenum as well as water-cooled turbo bearing housing—both these features increase the drivability and increase peace of mind when piling up those cruise miles.

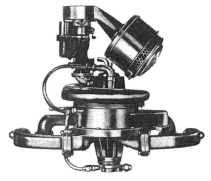

Besasie-Chevrolet turbocharger circa 1949. Note compactness of design with integrated intake and exhaust manifolds.

Besasie turbocharger installed on a Powerglide 1950 Chevrolet. 6 pounds of boost gave 155 HP.

Simple J pipe connects the stock exhaust manifold to the bottom of the TO4.

see an airplane with a Roots type of supercharger!" The best compressor is the one that heats the air the least for the pounds of boost produced and here is where turbos win hands down, and they don't tap 50–100 horsepower off the front of the crankshaft. For every pound of boost, there is an approximate

10 percent increase in horsepower at the rear wheels! You want to match the turbocharger to the octane you're using, the higher the octane, the higher the boost. Even at 87 octane, you can effect a 6-pound boost safely (if the proper compression ratio, fuel calibration and spark are applied). If you live in a high altitude locale or one where the ambient temperature is likely to routinely be 100F, you need to add an intercooler.

There are too many advantages to this path to power to let misinformation and fear stop us. Let's pause for a moment and analyze what keeps most people from building a turbocharged inline.

Turbo Lag—This can be controlled by proper turbo sizing, converter selection, transmission selection, and final drive ratio. What you want, at least for the street, is to set the boost to come in at 2000 RPM in high gear (not overdrive).

Turbo Selection—This seems like a black art to many and it is a place where expensive mistakes can occur. Always do your homework first by gaining as much knowledge as possible. I would suggest you start by reading *Maximum Boost* by Corky Bell. Second, find someone knowledgeable and trustworthy like Ak Miller and thoroughly discuss your contemplated plan.

Draw-Through/Blow-Through—You need to decide whether to put the carburetor before the turbo and draw air through it or force the air through the carburetor after it leaves the turbo.

Drawing the air through results in a simple, very compact arrangement for our inline engines, eliminates the need for a separate compressor waste gate and requires no carburetor

John Broden's immaculate STD-LD turbo powered 1938 Chevy coupe.

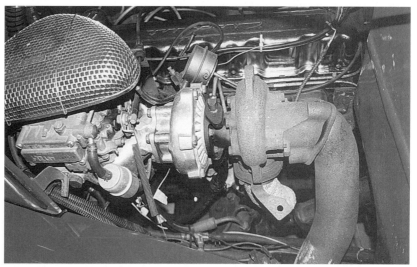

STD-LD "250" features a TO3 in a draw-through system headed by a 600 CFM Holley carburetor. Note the almost stock factory-like appearance of this compact system.

Bottom end remains stock. Mild head work (center intake bosses streamlined but not removed), Fel-Pro® 1025 head gasket (no O-ring of block or head)—studs are used. Camshaft is a Crower hydraulic with stock lifters and pushrods. John reports the short block has over 200,000 miles on it!

TURBOCHARGED HORSEPOWER POTENTIAL L6

ENGINE SIZE	LOW HP HIGH HP			POUNDS OF BOOST		
			STREET		COMPETITION	
STD-LD		6	8	10	15	20	30

ENGINE SIZE	LOW HP HIGH HP	6	8	10	15	20	30
230	L	248	271	295	355	415	535
	H	367	402	437	526	614	792
250	L	269	295	321	386	451	581
	H	398	437	475	572	668	860
258	L	277	304	331	398	465	599
	H	411	451	491	590	689	888
HD - TD							
292	L	314	345	375	451	527	679
	H	465	510	555	668	780	1005
301	L	324	355	387	465	543	700
	H	480	526	573	688	804	1036

FORMULA
L .052 x Displacement x (Boost + 14.7)
H .077 x Displacement x (Boost + 14.7)

REFERENCE: *Maximum Boost* by Corky Bell

STD-LD and HD-TD horsepower potential related to boost.

Gary White's backyard turbocharged STD-LD dragster.

modifications other than a richer air fuel ratio. In the practical world, this setup still produces startling results. The big disadvantage is it precludes the use of an intercooler.

The other option is to take maximum advantage of turbo boost by incorporating an intercooler and forcing the air through the carburetor (which requires specifically modified carburetors or a carburetor enclosure) and more elaborate tubing configuration and a more spread-out design incorporating a waste gate.

Most experts would argue this is a no-brainer because the blow-through systems with intercooler give more throttle response, reduced emissions, better cold weather starting and about 30 percent increase in horsepower. In an ideal world, this is the system to use.

Boost Control—A turbocharger has an interesting characteristic: it can increase its rate of airflow vs. RPM faster than the engine can accept it. So, if you don't control this tendency in some proactive way, the boost pressure will go out of sight and our engine will self-destruct.

A device called a *waste gate* provides this protective function. It does that by letting a percentage of the exhaust energy bypass the turbo. The simplest waste gates are made integral to the turbo; however, a remote waste gate is a must in racing applications, as integral waste gates are simply too small. The waste gate is the most important tool in eliminating turbo lag. It allows you to size the turbo for excellent low-speed boost and response and yet not over-boost at higher RPM.

Detonation Controls—Forced air induction magnifies potential problems with detonation. This is controlled by keeping your compression ratio

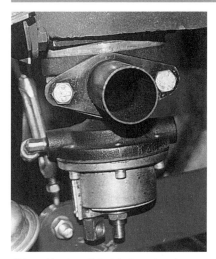

Driver side view. Note tubular exhaust manifold with waste gate attached to the bottom plenum.

Draw-through using a Quadra-jet four-barrel carburetor and a turbo pirated from a John Deere tractor. The engine is a "258" and is blowing into a Clifford intake manifold. Driver side view.

lower than normal and your fuel octane high, with an intercooler to lower inlet temperature and by matching ignition timing to the fuel curve. Remember, the turbo mixture burns faster than an atmospheric mixture, therefore boosted engines require less spark advance. By using not only a vacuum advance in the distributor, but also a pressure retard and knock sensor, you can create a safe engine environment.

For a draw-through system, or if an intercooler is impractical, then serious consideration must be given to a water injection system—even if it is as unsophisticated as a windshield washer pump (and fluid) injecting into the primaries of the carburetor! The use of approximately 10–20 percent injection rate works well. The final rate must be determined by trial and error.

Turbo Checklist

1. Arm yourself with knowledge before you begin your project. There are at least three books you should have: *Maximum Boost,* by Corky Bell, Robert Bentley Automotive Publishers;

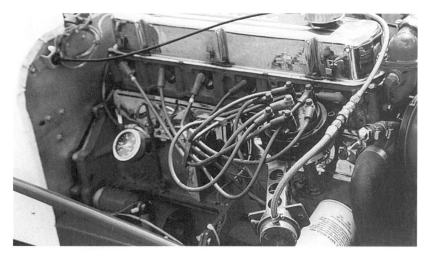

Note the use of a pressure retard on the distributor.

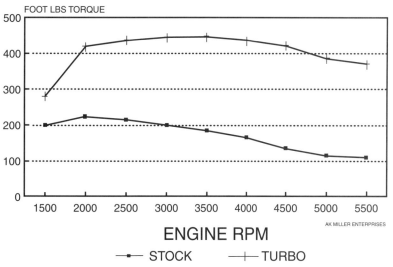

250 CUBIC INCH L6 CYLINDER
TURBOCHARGED - 13 LBS. BOOST
STOCK 239° CAMSHAFT - PROPANE FUEL

AK MILLER ENTERPRISES

Dyno-test—Ak Miller STD-LD.

Harry Stirnemann's beautiful 1937 Chevy coupe. Turbocharged HD-TD. Runs the quarter in 10.13 at 130 MPH in street trim.

Draw-through system features a highly modified 900 CFM Holley carburetor on a Turbonetics 60-1 turbocharger.

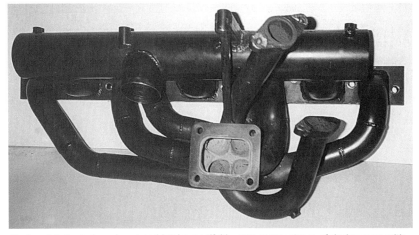

Custom tubular turbo exhaust and intake manifold—note compactness of design even with twin waste gates.

Turbochargers, by Hugh MacInnes, HP Books Putnam Berkley Publishing; and *Super Power,* by Larry Schreib, Car Tech/SA Design.

2. Size the turbo to the engine and horsepower projection.
3. Intercool.
4. Low compression 8.5 to 1 allows more boost with less chance of detonation.
5. Mild cam timing. Stock cam for street use. Special turbo cam (short duration, high lift, minimum overlap) for full competition use.
6. Head studs and Fel-Pro® 1025 head gasket for the street. O-ring the block and use stainless wire with either a Detroit gasket or dead-soft copper head gasket for full competition.
7. Stock cast exhaust manifold HD-TD 2-1/2" diameter outlet for street. Short stainless tubular headers for competition.
8. Large exhaust 3"–4" diameter after turbo.
9. Correct air/fuel ratio (11 to 1 at full throttle) and ignition curve.
10. Minimal headwork for street. High flow porting for competition.
11. When using the blow-through system: Offenhauser or Clifford four-barrel ram flow manifolds are best for street. For competition, with lump port intake, use Precision Engine Service ram four-barrel design if space permits, or have Inline Engine Performance Products make a custom manifold for you.
12. Water injection to suppress detonation, especially in a draw-through system.

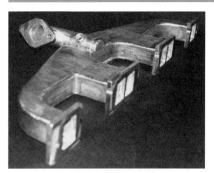

Inline Engine Performance's custom stainless exhaust manifold for TO4 split scroll turbo and competition waste gate (Top view).

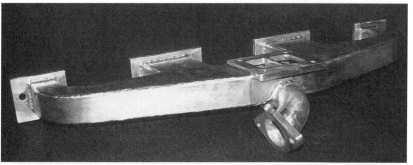

Bottom view.

Air Research split scroll TO4 turbocharger.

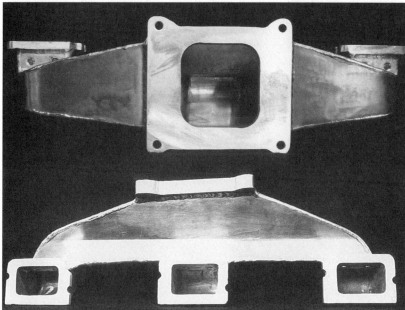

Inline Engine Performance's custom high ram effect aluminum four-barrel manifold to be used in a blow-through application. Note injector holes so that it may be used with constant flow port fuel injection in the style of Ron's "Four Shooter" design.

Turbonetics competition waste gate.

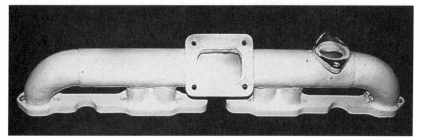

Custom heavy tubular exhaust manifold by Ak Miller provides turbo and waste gate mountings in a very compact package for the hybrid head HD-TD engine.

Close-up of the smooth 3" diameter exit from the turbo. The exhaust manifold can sometimes pose a packaging challenge with the firewall in some installations.

Leo Santucci's turbocharged 1950 Chevy coupe HD-TD with hybrid head conversion ran 10.25 at 130 MPH in the quarter mile off the trailer.

Blow-through system utilizes intercooler between the turbo and the intake manifold. Note hybrid head conversion and constant flow port fuel injection.

Garrett TO4 turbo. Note large area air filter to support this engine's 600 horsepower.

Chapter 16

What About Nitrous Oxide?

- Why nitrous is similar to super- and turbocharging
- Nicknamed chemical supercharging or chemcharging

Suppose you could add 75–125 HP to your inline at the touch of a button and make no interior changes to your engine? Would that be great or what? Suppose it were also quite cost-effective to purchase such a system and the installation was very straight-forward? And what if that system didn't make your engine less driveable? Do I have your attention?

History

In 1772, Joseph Priestly was the first person to derive nitrous oxide. He also discovered oxygen—that's why the name sounded familiar, from junior high school science class—or, was that the class you slept through?

Nitrous oxide is a colorless gas that is heavier than air and has slightly sweet odor and taste. By the 1800s, it became medicine's first anesthesia. You probably remember it as laughing gas. Dentists used it widely in the early part of the 20th century for its anesthetic properties, until they discovered its potentially deadly side effects. Today, medical grade nitrous oxide is highly regulated for that reason.

It is unclear who discovered the use of nitrous as a fuel additive, but because it carries

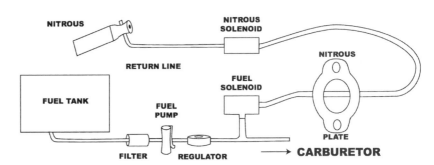

SINGLE BARREL

NITROUS SYSTEM
DEADHEAD REGULATOR

The typical nitrous system utilizes a stock carburetor and homemade injector plate. This works well with single or dual single-barrel carburetion. About a 50 to 75 horsepower improvement can be achieved.

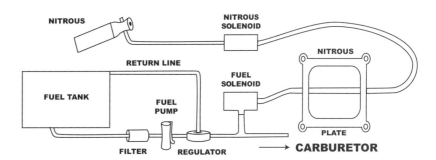

FOUR BARREL

NITROUS SYSTEM
WITH BYPASS REGULATOR

Nitrous system utilizing either a single four-barrel or dual four-barrel. Note bypass fuel regulator—a preferred method for high horsepower applications.

Nitrous system plumbed to a Holley two-barrel carburetor mounted on an older 12-port GMC engine.

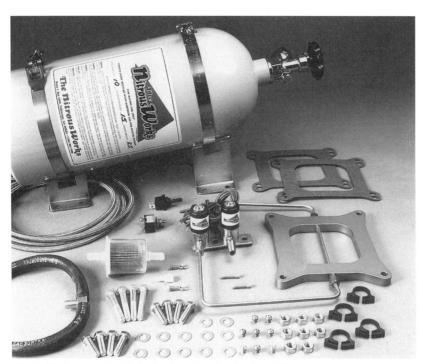

Nitrous Works' complete kit for four-barrel application (Part #PN10010) makes an excellent place to start your nitrous adventure.

oxygen within the molecule, and is combustible, it wasn't long before experiments were going on.

The first general use of nitrous oxide in internal combustion engines was in World War II when it came into wide use in fighter planes, particularly by the Germans and British. It gave a power boost and assisted in high altitude maneuvers and reconnaissance. As the war ended and jet aircraft came into prominence, nitrous oxide was dropped as an automotive oxidizer because, even in condensed form, it took too much volume to package.

Some racers experimented with crude systems up through the '50s by adding nitrous to gasoline-powered engines. By the mid to late '60s, racers had figured out how to use unrefined systems and those who knew "the secret" had a tremendous advantage in both drag and oval track competition.

Concealed systems were run by some of the top names before the rules makers put an end to it. Nitrous development has continued and it has become a very refined way to get a healthy boost of power.

Probably the largest group of nitrous users are street racers and street rodders, and with good reason—nitrous works perfectly on "dual purpose" cars. You end up with the best of both worlds—smooth engine characteristics for cruising, and, at the punch of a button, you've got an extra 100 horsepower. To top it all off, compared with the modifications necessary to get 100 horsepower by camming, compression, etc., modern nitrous systems are economical to purchase and can be moved from one car to another.

If nitrous has a downside, it is that the power increase is all or nothing. The engine must be at full throttle before the nitrous is engaged. This is different from a turbo or blower, where near full throttle and short-shifting techniques can give a more relaxed power boost that's useful for street driving. Having to fill the bottle after approximately three to five minutes worth of boost is also a factor.

Discussion

Nitrous oxide, or N_2O, is not used as a fuel when we apply it to engines; it is just another, more convenient way to increase the oxygen in the fuel/air mixture. After all, everything we do to increase the power level of these engines revolves around pumping in more fuel and air. Hence, we port and polish, use more radical cam timing,

increase the cubic inches and use better flowing carbs and manifolds, etc. Well, N_2O contains about 35 percent oxygen, while regular air contains only about 22 percent oxygen. So, doesn't it make sense to use this trick to add power? Now, how do we get the oxygen from the nitrogen? The heat of the combustion process breaks the chemical bonds and releases the oxygen in the process but it takes almost 600F to accomplish this. Once we have the extra oxygen

released, we must increase our fuel flow to compensate or a very lean burn will occur leading to detonation and certain engine destruction.

Many tests have led most nitrous suppliers to tailor their systems to provide an additional part of fuel for each 9.5 parts of nitrous oxide. This extra fuel often is planned as a separate system, controlled with solenoids and relays to work automatically when you hit the "GO" button.

The ultimate in nitrous carburetor systems shown here on an STD-LD engine—Triple Weber 45 DCOEs. Note additional fuel enrichment lines.

Venom—the first of a new generation of nitrous kits that are fully computer programmable.

Why Nitrous

When all of this is set up correctly, a nitrous-injected engine will create horsepower increases in a way few other modifications can. Power is made through more efficient combustion at RPM levels that allow an inline engine to thrive within its design limits. Stop and think a minute—how long do you think an inline engine will last if you don't have to rev it above 6000 RPM?

If nitrous sounds like it makes sense to you, the next step is to read as much as you can on the subject. The following books will be helpful: *Super Power* by Larry Schreib, *Nitrous Racing* by Alex Walordy, *N₂O Power* by Alex Walordy.

Instruction manuals from the various manufacturers are also helpful, as well as a discussion with a technical representative. Companies to consider are the following:

1. NOS (Nitrous Oxide Systems, Inc.)
2. Nitrous Works
3. Python Injection, Inc. (makers of Venom, the first computerized nitrous system)

The most common and easily adapted nitrous systems use a plate that bolts between the carburetor and the intake manifold. This plate contains spray bars to deliver both nitrous and additional fuel when called upon. As far as I know, no company supplies a plate for a one-barrel carburetor. You would have to use a universal kit and make (or have fabricated) a delivery plate. This should be relatively straightforward using an old phenolic carb insulator. Of course, if you have modified your engine, and have a four-barrel intake, then most nitrous manufacturers can supply a bolt-on plate and system. For all-out racing, nitrous nozzles can be fit closer to the intake ports (these nozzles are similar to fuel injection nozzles) and you may use multi-stage timed nitrous controllers to provide maximum useable power at predetermined RPM ranges.

Important Notes

1. Be careful handling nitrous. It is extremely cold and can easily cause "burns" similar to frostbite.
2. Always start with a moderate approach. Don't expect to add 200 HP to a stock short-block and expect it to survive!
3. Always err on the side of a richer fuel/nitrous mixture and gradually tune to optimal power levels.
4. Typically, nitrous engines do not need as much spark advance as atmospheric engines. This is due to the increased pressure that builds in each cylinder during the combustion process. Be conservative. Err on the side of less advance. Start with 2° retarded from your regular atmospheric baseline and tune from there. Detonation leads to extensive and expensive repairs!
5. Expect an improvement in quarter mile times of between .5 and 2 seconds and 8–12 miles per hour depending on other engine and drive-line modifications.
6. Use only premium octane fuel on the street. When racing, use appropriate octane racing fuel.
7. Stock camshafts work well in street applications. Further power can be gained with a nitrous grind for more serious power.
8. Listen to your technical advisor. When in doubt, ask for help.
9. Have fun!

ATI Performance Products, Inc
(dampers)
6747 White Stone Road
Baltimore, MD 21207
410-298-4343
www.atiperformanceproducts.com

ATI/Procharger
Accessible Technologies, Inc.
(centrifugal superchargers and intercoolers)
14801 W. 114th Terrace
Lenexa, KS 66215
913-338-2886
www.procharger.com

Arias Racing Pistons
13420 S. Normandie Avenue
Gardena, CA 90249
310-532-9737
www.ariaspistons.com

Automotive Racing Products (ARP)
531 Spectrum Circle
Oxnard, CA 93030
800-826-3045
805-278-7223

Aviaid Oil Systems
10041 Canoga Ave.
Chatsworth, CA 91311
818-998-8991
www.aviaid.com

BHJ Products—Honing Plates
37530 Enterprise Court, #3
Newark, CA 94560
510-797-6780
www.bhjinc.com

Blown Plum Crazy
Gail Plummer
3135 SW Raleigh View Drive
Portland, OR 97225
503-292-5516

Bow Tie Speed & Reproduction
4 Main Street
La Fargeville, NY 13656
315-658-2053

Canton Racing Products
232 Branford Road
North Branford, CT 06471
203-481-9460

Clark Copper Head Gaskets, Inc.
10510 Nassau Street NE
Blaine, MN 55449
763-786-9590

Clifford Performance
2330 Pomona-Rincon Road
Corona, CA 92880
909-734-3310
www.cliffordperformance.com

Cloyes Gear & Products
615 West Walnut
Paris, AR 72855
501-963-2105
www.cloyes.com

Comp Cams
3406 Democrat Road
Memphis, TN 38118
800-999-0853
www.compcams.com

Crane Cams
(also Wolverine Blue Racer)
530 Fentress Boulevard
Daytona Beach, FL 32114
386-252-1151
www.cranecams.com

Crankshaft Specialists
280 Tillman
Memphis, TN 38112
901-452-6663
www.crankshaftspecialists.com

K.J. Crawford, Inc.—Fuel Injection
1575 Marlow Road
Santa Rosa, CA 95401
707-542-9551

Crower Cams & Equipment
3333 Main Street
Chula Vista, CA 91911-5899
619-422-1191
www.crower.com

Custom Design Performance
219 Route 6
Columbia, CT 06237
860-228-3449
www.cdpautomachine.com

Delta Cams
Jerry Bodwell
1938 Tacoma Avenue South
Tacoma, WA 98402
800-562-5500

Edelbrock
2700 California Street
Torrance, CA 90503
800-416-8628

Enderle Fuel Injection
1830 N. Voyager Avenue
Simi Valley, CA 93063
805-526-3838

Fel-Pro®
Federal Mogul
www.federal-mogul.com/felpro

Fisher Concepts
10640 S. Garfield Avenue
South Gate, CA 90280
562-861-6882
www.fisherconcepts.com

Fluidampr
11980 Walden Avenue
Alden, NY 14004
716-937-3603

Fontana Automotive, Inc.
13630 S. St. Andrews Pl.
Gardena, CA 90249
310-538-2505

Garrett® Engine Boosting Systems
3201 W. Lomita Blvd.
Torrance, CA 90505-5064
www.egarrett.com

GRP Connecting Rods
2200 S. Jason Street
Denver, CO 80223
303-935-7565
www.grpconrods.com

Hilborn Fuel Injection Engineering
22892 Glenwood Drive
Aliso Viego, CA 92656
949-360-0909
www.hilborninjection.com

Hogan's Racing Manifolds
303 N. Russell Ave.
Santa Maria, CA 93458
805-928-8483
www.hogansracingmanifolds.com

Holley Carburetors
1801 Russellville Road
Bowling Green, KY 42102
207-781-9741
www.holley.com

Inline Engine Performance
Ed Eichholz
2010 Marsh Road
Wilmington, DE 19810
302-475-4614

Iskenderian Racing Cams
1620 S. Broadway
Gardena, CA 90248
323-770-0930
www.iskycam.com

JE Pistons
15312 Connector Lane
Huntington Beach, CA 92649
714-898-9763
www.jepistons.com

Joe Hunt Magnetos
11336 A Sunco Drive
Rancho Cordova, CA 95742
916-635-5387
www.huntmagnetos.com

Kansas Kustoms & Klassics
113 E. Sherman
Hutchinson, KS 16701
316-663-3256

Kinsler Fuel Injection
1834A Thunderbird
Troy, MI 48084
248-362-1145
www.kinsler.com

Langdon's Stovebolt Engine Parts Co.
47950 Robin Street
Utica, MI 48317
810-739-9601
www.stoveboltengineco.com

MSD Ignition
1490 Henry Brennan Drive
El Paso, TX 79936
915-857-5200
www.msdignition.com

Manley Performance
1960 Swarthmore Avenue
Lakewood, NJ 08701
732-905-3366

AK Miller Enterprises
9256 Bermudez Street
Pico Rivera, CA 90660
562-949-8333

Moon Racing Cams
Bill Jenks
10820 S. Norwalk Boulevard
Santa Fe Springs, CA 90670
562-944-6311
www.mooneyes.com

Moroso Performance
80 Carter Drive
Guilford, CT 06437
203-453-6571
www.moroso.com

Mr. Gasket
550 Mallory Way
Carson City, NV 89701
775-882-6600
www.mrgasket.com

Nitrous Oxide Systems
1357 E. Grand Avenue
Pomona, CA 91766
714-545-0580
www.nosnitrous.com

Nitrous Works
1450 McDonald Road
Dahlonega, GA 30533
706-864-7009
www.barrygrant.com

Offenhauser Sales Corp.
PO Box 32219
Los Angeles, CA 90032
323-225-1307

Paxton Automotive
2146 Eastman Avenue
Oxnard, CA 93030
888-972-9866
www.paxtonauto.com

Pertronix Inc.
440 E. Arrow Highway
San Dimas, CA 91773
800-827-3758
www.pertronix.com

Powerdyne™ Superchargers
104C East Avenue K-4
Lancaster, CA 93535
661-723-2800
www.powerdyne.com

Predator Carburetors
810 Cross Street
Lakewood, NJ 08701
732-367-8487
www.predatorcarb.com

Precision Engine Service
Clyde Norwood
2511 Providence Road, South
Waxhaw, NC 28173
704-843-5477

Python Injection, Inc.
8625 Central Avenue
Stanton, CA 90680
800-959-2865
www.python-injection.com

RAM Clutches
201 Business Park Boulevard
Columbia, SC 29203
803-788-6034
www.ramclutches.com

Race Engine Design
770 Chickamanga Avenue
Rossville, GA 30741
706-866-3000

Robert Bentley, Publishers
1033 Massachusetts Avenue
Cambridge, MA 02138
800-423-4595
www.bentleypublishers.com

Ron's Fuel Injection
3249 E. Milbar
Tucson, AZ 85714
800-513-3835

Ross Racing Pistons
625 S. Douglas Street
El Segundo, CA 90245
310-536-0100
www.rosspistons.com

Self Racing Heads & Engines
Glen Self, Kevin Self
54 W. Locust
Durant, OK 74701
580-924-5866
www.selfracing.com

Sissell's Automotive
Mike Kirby
1463 Virginia Avenue
Baldwin Park, CA 91706
626-960-1090

Smith Brothers Pushrods
1320 S.E. Armour Road A-1
Bend, OR 97702
800-367-1533
www.pushrods.net

SCE Gaskets, Inc.
1122 West Avenue L-12, Suite 108
Lancaster, CA 93534
800-427-5380
www.scegaskets.com

Super Speed Equipment Co., Inc.
Former manufacturer of Superods
No longer in production

System One Filtration®
P.O. Box 1097
Tulare, CA 93275
559-687-1955
www.system1filter.com

TCI Automotive
151 Industrial Drive
Ashland, MS 38603
662-224-8972
www.tciauto.com

TD Performance Products
16410 Manning Way
Cerritos, CA 90703
562-921-0404
www.tdperformance.com

Total Seal Piston Rings
22642 N. 15th Avenue
Phoenix, AZ 85027
800-874-2753
www.totalseal.com

Turbonetics
2255 Agate Court
Simi Valley, CA 93065
805-581-0333
www.turboneticsinc.com

Ultradyne Cams
7173-302 Industrial Drive
Southaven, MS 38671
662-349-4447
www.ultradyne.com

Venolia Pistons
2160 Cherry Industrial Circle
Long Beach, CA 90805
323-636-9329
email: venolia@aol.com

Vertex Magnetos
Taylor Vertex
301 Highgrove Road
Grandview, MO 64030
800-821-3600
www.taylorvertex.com

Vortech Engineering
1650 Pacific Avenue
Channel Islands, CA 93033-9901
805-247-0226
www.vortechsuperchargers.com

Wiseco Piston, Inc.
7201 Industrial Park Boulevard
Mentor, OH 44060
800-321-1364

Yother Automotive
1740 Timothy Drive
San Leandro, CA 94577
800-446-9094